CRIME FILES

CRIME FILES

CHILLING CASE STUDIES OF HUMAN DEPRAVITY

JOHN MARLOWE

ARCTURUS

ARCTURUS

This edition published in 2012 by Arcturus Publishing Limited
26/27 Bickels Yard, 151–153 Bermondsey Street,
London SE1 3HA

ISBN: 978-1-84837-148-4
AD000131EN

Printed in Singapore

CONTENTS

INTRODUCTION

File folders, thousands of them, can be found in even the smallest of police stations. Typically, they're housed in desk drawers, filing cabinets and vast rooms overseen by records clerks who are specially entrusted and trained for the task. The vast majority of the files that these men and women receive concern the mundane: incident reports, supplemental reports, accident reports, pawn tickets, warrants, arrest sheets, custody sheets, property sheets and on it goes. However, every once in a while, a clerk will handle files containing information that has made headlines the world over.

We outside law enforcement may have some idea, however skewed, of police work through the media and crime shows on television, but we remain largely unaware of the vast amount of paper that is consumed by criminal acts and subsequent investigations.

Consider the case – or cases – against Carl Panzram, as an example. His recorded criminal history begins near the close of the 19th century, when at the age of 8, he was picked up by police for being drunk in a public place. Over the three decades that followed, Panzram was arrested on at least eight other occasions. The multitude of crimes he committed, ranging from burglary and arson to rape and multiple murder, was investigated by a number of police departments. Files on his various crimes can be found in the states of Minnesota, Oregon, New York, Massachusetts, Connecticut, Maryland, Pennsylvania and Kansas. Panzram himself added a great deal of material to his files by writing an autobiography while in prison. This remarkable 20,000-word document is not only much more extensive and detailed than any of the confessions he'd previously provided for law enforcement officials, but it also contains information on crimes that had eluded investigation. Writing the memoir was, perhaps, the most honest act the criminal ever committed.

Panzram was eventually hanged for his manifold crimes. The last words he uttered were addressed to his executioner: 'Hurry it up, you Hoosier bastard! I could kill ten men while you're fooling around.'

This unpleasant encounter on the scaffold took place in 1930. Despite the efforts of a good many people – including Henry Lesser, a prison guard who befriended Panzram – it wasn't until 1976 that the murderer's memoir was allowed to be published. *The Carl Panzram Papers*, Lesser's own collection of writing by and about the man, can be found at San Diego State University – yet another crime file.

Panzram, the earliest criminal covered in these pages, has something in common with the most recent, Anders Breivik, in that they both contributed damning writing to their respective files.

The latter's 1,513-page *2083 – A European Declaration of Independence*, provides details not only of his motives, but the considerable preparations undertaken in order to commit mass murder. Part-manifesto, part-confession, the document has also shown itself to be in large measure a work of plagiarism.

Breivik lifted whole sections from works that are properly attributed to the American Free Congress Foundation, far-right blogger Peder Jenson, and Unabomber Ted Kaczynski. However, charges of plagiarism don't even register when placed beside Breivik's other crimes.

In contrast to the Panzram manuscript, there was no decades-long wait for those curious about *2083*.

In fact, Breivik posted the entire document online just before he began his killing spree.

In this digital age, police departments routinely produce documentation on paper, while increasingly finding evidence in digital form. For example, in November 2009, disgraced Canadian Forces colonel Russell Williams left a threatening message on a victim's home computer. Three months later, police searching the murderer's Ottawa home uncovered several hidden flash drives that contained evidence of his crimes.

Stephen Griffiths, England's self-proclaimed 'Crossbow Cannibal', had a very active online presence. Sitting in his bachelor apartment, calling himself 'Ven Pariah', he visited social networking sites, at which he described himself as a demon. Griffiths also maintained a macabre website, called 'The Skeleton and the Jaguar', devoted largely to serial killers. Two of his murderous attacks were recorded digitally. The most famous, captured by a closed circuit camera in the hallway of his block of flats, resulted in his arrest and was broadcast around the world. The second, a horrific scene, Griffiths recorded on his mobile phone. Viewed by only a few people involved with the investigation, the images were destroyed after the Crossbow Cannibal pleaded guilty and was sentenced.

The criminal acts here reach back nearly one hundred years. They begin at a time before most people had access to photography and end at a time in which murderers have Facebook accounts. Whether earlier days were safer days may be a matter for debate, but they were certainly easier to stomach.

John Marlowe
Montreal, Quebec, Canada

Carl Panzram

THE COLONEL'S DARK SECRET

Russell Williams

Name: Russell Williams

DOB: 7 March 1963

Profession: Colonel in the Canadian armed forces

Previous convictions: None

Number of victims: 2

In May 2005, Russell Williams, a respected member of the Canadian armed forces, commanded flights carrying Queen Elizabeth and Prince Philip during the royal couple's tour of Canada. He performed similar functions for prime ministers Paul Martin and Stephen Harper. Williams' public persona played on duty, responsibility and trust, all of which would prove to be misplaced.

David Russell Williams was born on 7 March 1963 in Cardiff, Wales, but lived – and will live – nearly his entire life in Canada. Though shaken by his parents' divorce, and his mother's subsequent marriage to a family friend, his upbringing was otherwise comfortable. He attended both public and private schools, ending his education in 1986 with a BA in Economics and Political Science from the University of Toronto. The graduate's next move came as a surprise to even his closest friends. Influenced by the newly released *Top Gun,* starring Tom Cruise as a cocky fighter pilot, Williams joined the Canadian armed forces. To some, this sudden change in direction seemed surreal; Williams had never before expressed any interest in the military.

Yet, in the face of his friends' misgivings, Williams took to this new career path. In 1990, he earned his wings, and on New Year's Day 1991 was promoted to captain. Over a 23-year military career, Williams was given increasingly important responsibilities. He piloted jets carrying VIPs, served as Director General Military Careers and was made commander of the 437 Squadron. Following a six-month tour in the

Persian Gulf, where he was in charge of the Theatre Support Element at the secretive Camp Mirage, Williams was posted to the Department of National Defence Headquarters in Ottawa.

The perfect package

Williams rose to the level of colonel, and in July 2009 was appointed commanding officer of Canadian Forces Base (CFB) Trenton in Ontario, Canada's largest air force base. To his superiors, Williams seemed to be the perfect package. He was considered a good leader, someone who was well organized and adept at administration. Lieutenant General Angus Watt, then the commanding officer of Canada's air force, described Williams as 'unusually calm, very logical, very rational'. The colonel was also recognized as a man who was extremely comfortable in speaking to the media.

This last feature was particularly important to the brass. During the war in Afghanistan, CFB Trenton served as the departure point for soldiers going overseas. It was at the base that the men and women serving in Afghanistan would take their final steps on Canadian soil... and it was here that the fallen would return. The responsibility was heavy, but the job was not without its perks. As commander, Williams had living accommodation on the base. This comfortable abode became his third home. He owned a cottage – more of a small house, really – on Cozy Cove Lane in Tweed, a pretty town of 5,000 or so inhabitants, about an hour's drive northeast of Trenton. Situated on a lakefront property, it offered a lovely view of picturesque Stoco Lake. But Williams didn't get out on the water often. His neighbour, Larry Jones, remembers the colonel as a busy man, someone who would be coming in and out at all hours. 'This guy comes in in the dark and leaves in the dark. Never see him. He has a controller for his garage — just slides right in. I figured, "Well, that guy's a busy man — base commander and all."'

The colonel's wife, Mary-Elizabeth Harriman, would usually stay at the third Williams home in Ottawa. Being partway between Trenton and the national capital, the cottage served as a meeting point for a couple that spent much more time apart than together.

Position of trust: Williams was in control of flying dignitaries across Canada

To at least a few friends, their relationship appeared slightly odd. Williams had had one – and only one – girlfriend while attending university. When that relationship ended, he did not date for nearly a decade. To even his closest friends, Williams' 1991 marriage appeared to have come out of the blue.

Strange compulsion

Williams' wife would come to the Cozy Cove cottage on weekends – but not with any great frequency. It seems unlikely that she would have been in Tweed on the autumn 2007 weekend when her husband first planted the seed of fear in the small town. There was little concern at first; a young woman had returned home to find a tall figure in jogging clothes attempting to break into her house. Whoever it was had been scared away. Just a neighbourhood kid was the thought.

No one suspected the colonel. However, it wasn't long before other break-ins, *successful* break-ins, were reported. The intruder appeared to have no interest in money, jewellery or electronics; it was women's intimate apparel, swimsuits and shoes that were being stolen. Williams would break, enter and steal from over 42 different Tweed homes, sometimes hitting two in a single evening. Among the houses he entered were the three immediately to the south of his cottage. There were times that the violations were obvious, but in many cases Williams took pains to leave no sign of his crimes.

Although no one made the link at the time, the Tweed break-ins were not dissimilar to those that had been taking place three hours away around his Ottawa home. In January 2007, he entered a nearby house, stole underwear belonging to a teenage girl and left what was described as 'DNA evidence' on the bureau. Before the end of 2009, Williams made

at least two dozen similar neighbourhood break-ins.

More than a thousand articles of clothing were stolen. The community grew tense, with many people fearful for their safety and that of their loved ones.

The concern was understandable; the break-ins were increasing in frequency. In the two months that followed Williams' promotion to commander of CFB Trenton, no fewer than ten Tweed homes were broken into. For those investigating the crimes, it was all so predictable. Lingerie, swimsuits, shoes and robes were stolen, along with the occasional photograph; DNA evidence was sometimes left behind.

However, on 17 September 2009, just hours after his return from a trip to the high Arctic, Williams' routine underwent a dramatic and disturbing change. Not long after midnight, a young Tweed mother was awoken by a masked intruder. Over a two-hour period, she was sexually assaulted, threatened and photographed. The woman's 8-week-old baby, asleep nearby, was unharmed during the ordeal.

The following evening, as police were investigating the assault, Williams returned to the home and, incredibly, broke into the very home in which the sexual assaults had occurred. A week later, after having spent the day at CFB Trenton with the Minister of Defence, Peter MacKay, he broke into the house a third time.

With the sexual assault, Williams' deviant pattern had changed. Before the month was out, the colonel repeatedly broke into a house not far from his cottage. It was not until his third home invasion that he encountered anyone. Like the first – like all of them – Williams' victim was a woman. She was home alone when he broke in. Threatening her, Williams

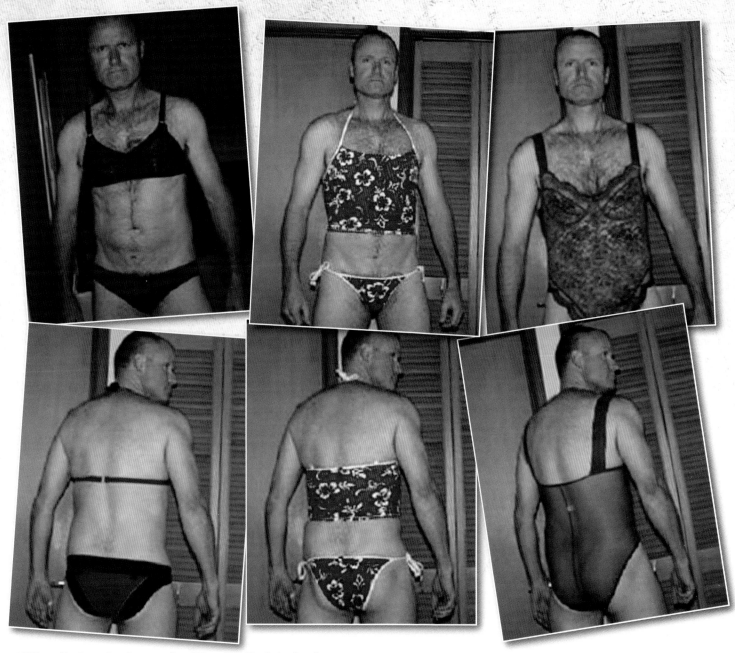

Williams liked to take photographs of himself in his victims' underwear

placed a blindfold over the woman's eyes, bound her to a chair and then cut off her clothes. Over the next two and a half hours, she was choked, beaten, sexually assaulted and photographed. Throughout the waking nightmare, the victim thought that she recognized the voice of her assailant.

By the morning, little Tweed had become a focus of the Ontario Provincial Police. Cozy Cove Lane was blanketed by investigators, but Williams wasn't at home. It hardly mattered. Once investigating officers learned that he was commander of CFB Trenton, he was considered above suspicion. Instead, they set their sights on Williams' next-door neighbour, Larry Jones, who owned one of the homes that had not reported a break-in. The second sexual assault victim had guessed that the voice she recognized belonged to Jones. Weeks passed before he was cleared.

As his neighbour came under investigation, the path Williams was heading down became even darker. In mid-November, he broke into the home of a woman who taught music at CFB Trenton. The colonel stole underwear and sex toys, and left an intimidating message on her computer. His victim later realized that she and Williams had been in the house at the same time. In a way, she'd been lucky.

> **Williams broke into the home of a woman who taught music at CFB Trenton. He stole underwear and sex toys, and left an intimidating message on her computer**

Williams' next victim, Marie France Comeau, also had links to CFB Trenton. A 38-year-old corporal in the armed forces, she lived in the nearby town of Brighton, a 15-minute commute from the base.

On 25 November, three days after she'd finished serving on a flight crew that had attended to Prime Minister Stephen Harper during a state visit to the Far East, Comeau's body was discovered in her home. She had been strangled.

That same day, Williams, as base commander, sent a letter to the murdered woman's family. 'Please let me know if there is anything I can do to help you', he wrote. However, his support only extended so far; the colonel did not attend the funeral.

It would only be a matter of weeks before Williams would kill again. His victim, 27-year-old Jessica Lloyd, lived alone on Highway 37 in a modest house that her murderer had passed dozens of times in driving between Trenton and Tweed.

Lloyd was last heard from on the evening of 28 January 2010, when she'd texted a friend goodnight. Nothing appeared at all unusual until the following morning when she failed to show up for work. A search of her house raised the level of concern; her identification, keys and cellphone were all accounted for.

The search for the missing woman lasted more than a week. It involved not only the local police, but the Search and Rescue team from CFB Trenton. Then, in the midst of the stubborn mystery, investigators caught a very lucky break. Two men reported that on the evening of the disappearance, they'd noticed an SUV parked in the middle of a field that bordered Lloyd's property. Though several days had passed, the SUV's tyre tracks – *distinctive* tyre tracks – remained preserved in the frozen snow.

A roadblock was set up along the highway. On 4 February, a week to the day after Lloyd was reported missing, Williams found himself amongst the hundreds of drivers on the receiving end of police questions. After a brief exchange, he was sent on his way. What the colonel didn't know was that in those few minutes he had become the prime suspect. From that point on, Williams was under police surveillance.

The police had, again, caught a lucky break. That day, Williams happened to be behind the wheel of his SUV, rather than his much-preferred BMW. After three days, police phoned Williams at his Orleans home, asking that he come to the Ottawa Police Service headquarters to answer questions. According to some reports, the colonel arrived thinking that the queries would be about Larry Jones, his neighbour.

The end of the game

Instead, the colonel was subjected to an interrogation conducted by Detective Sergeant Jim Smyth of the Ontario Provincial Police's Behavioural Science Unit. Recordings of the ten hours that followed are now studied by law enforcement officers the world over as an example of how to obtain a confession.

It was, in some ways, a psychological chess game in which a very intelligent man was outmanoeuvred by another. Yet Smyth was careful not to present himself as an opponent. Instead, he calmly presented layers of evidence, which all led to this fifth-hour exchange:

> **SMYTH:** *So what am I doing, Russ? I put my best foot forward here for you, bud. I really have. I don't know what else to do to make you understand the impact of what's happening here. Can we talk?*
> **WILLIAMS:** *I want to minimize the impact on my wife.*
> **SMYTH:** *So do I.*
> **WILLIAMS:** *So how do we do that?*
> **SMYTH:** *Well, you start by telling the truth.*
> **WILLIAMS:** *Okay.*
> **SMYTH:** *Okay. So where is she* [Jessica Lloyd]?
> **WILLIAMS:** *Got a map?*

Even as he was being interrogated, police acting on search warrants were combing through Williams' homes in Orleans and Tweed. They discovered the stolen underwear, bathing suits, robes and shoes. He'd grabbed pictures of several women and girls from whom he'd stolen the apparel. But there were more photographs: thousands of images Williams had taken of the two women he'd assaulted, along with the two he'd murdered. There were other photos he'd taken of himself wearing the stolen undergarments. The colonel had unwittingly made the investigation even easier with a notebook in which he'd recorded the dates and the addresses of his crimes, with an inventory of the items that he'd stolen.

The day after his interrogation and confession, Williams led police to Jessica Lloyd's body, which he'd dumped in a wooded area just ten minutes from the Cozy Cove cottage.

Williams was charged with two counts of first-degree murder, two counts of sexual assault, two charges of forcible confinement and 82 further charges relating to theft and breaking and entering. Awaiting his day in court, the colonel tried to commit suicide by stuffing a toilet paper roll down his throat, but was thwarted by prison guards.

On 22 October 2010, this man who had once been entrusted with the safety of Queen Elizabeth and Prince Philip received two life sentences for first-degree murder, four ten-year sentences for forcible confinement and sexual assault, and 82 one-year sentences for burglary. The same day, Williams was stripped of his commission, ranks and awards. In what is believed to be an unprecedented action, his uniform and medals were destroyed.

Breakthrough: Distinctive tyre tracks found at murder scene

Behaviour in court: Defeated

Statement of defence: 'Why? I don't know the answers. And I'm pretty sure the answers don't matter.'

Sentence: Two life sentences, four ten-year sentences and 82 one-year sentences

THE CROSSBOW CANNIBAL

Stephen Griffths

Name: Stephen Griffiths

DOB: 24 December 1969

Profession: Student

Aliases: The Crossbow Cannibal, The Lizard Man

Previous convictions: Assault, shoplifting

Number of victims: 3 (at least)

A psychology graduate and PhD student in Applied Criminal Justice Studies, Stephen Griffiths is destined to be remembered as 'The Crossbow Cannibal'. The gruesome moniker didn't come from the popular press, but from the man himself. On 28 May 2010, wearing a black shirt and jeans, he stood in a packed magistrates' court and boldly gave the name in place of his own.

The declaration was met with gasps from a crowd that had no idea what it was he had done with the three women he was accused of murdering. When asked by the court clerk for his address, the Crossbow Cannibal replied, 'Here, I guess.' These short lines were part of a three-minute performance that ended with the 40-year-old confirming his date of birth.

Stephen Shaun Griffiths was born in Dewsbury, West Yorkshire on 24 December 1969 – like all children, he couldn't wait for Christmas Day, went the family joke. The eldest of three children, Shaun, as he was known, was a slender child. The Crossbow Cannibal's first moniker was 'The Stickman'.

Unlike his siblings, Griffiths was introspective and quiet. 'You could never get a read on him,' remarked one uncle. 'He was very much a loner.'

Griffiths didn't seem to care much for football or any other interests of most boys his age. This is not to say that he didn't attract attention. One former neighbour recalls that as a child the future murderer had a habit of killing and dismembering birds: 'It looked as if he was enjoying what he was doing.

He wasn't dissecting them bit by bit, he was ripping them apart.'

In trouble

When Griffiths was still very young, his parents split up. He moved with his mother, sister and brother to the nearby city of Wakefield. There he attended the exclusive and expensive Queen Elizabeth Grammar School, the alma mater of serial killer John George Haigh, 'The Acid Bath Murderer'.

He was a diligent student, but outside school Griffiths was often in trouble with the law. In his early teens he was caught stealing from a garage. At the age of 17, he slashed a supermarket manager with a knife when he was stopped for shoplifting. Griffiths received a three-year sentence for that attack, some of which was spent at a high-security mental hospital. One doctor diagnosed Griffiths as a 'sadistic, schizoid psychopath'. Another recorded that the youth had a 'preoccupation with murder – particularly multiple murder'. Griffiths told his probation officer that he believed he would one day become a serial killer.

Within three years, Griffiths was back in prison, this time for holding a knife to the throat of a young girl. He could give no reason for his actions.

Not long after his release, the future Crossbow Cannibal got into trouble again, this time for possessing two airguns and carrying a knife in public. Despite his years of incarceration, further run-ins with the law and wildly unpredictable, anti-social behaviour, Griffiths managed to earn a degree in psychology from Leeds University. He was accepted at the University of Bradford, where he began six years of work on an academic thesis, 'Homicide in an Industrial City', comparing modern murder techniques in Bradford to those used during the second half of the 19th century. Griffiths incorporated some of his research in 'The Skeleton and the Jaguar', a website he established that focused largely on serial killers.

He spent a good amount of time online, frequenting social networking sites. Griffiths would identify himself as 'Ven Pariah... the misanthrope who brought hate into heaven', under which guise he would post his disturbing thoughts. 'Humanity', he once wrote, 'is not merely a biological condition. It is also a state of mind. On that basis, I am a pseudo-human at best. A demon at worst.'

His relationships with women

Photos released by the police of victims Susan Rushworth, Suzanne Blamires and Shelley Armitage

Things got so bad in the building where Griffiths lived that they fitted an emergency alarm

tended to be abusive and short-lived, yet he fathered at least one child. Griffiths was arrested numerous times for domestic violence, and once appeared in court for leaving threatening messages on the voicemail of a former girlfriend.

Sinister habits

From his teens on, Griffiths was one of those people the media describes as being 'known to police'. In 2008, attention increased after local librarians reported that he'd been borrowing books on human dismemberment. This warning sign coincided with problems at the building in which he rented a small bachelor flat. Male neighbours were being threatened, while the females increasingly became the focus of untoward attention. Two women reported that a once friendly and polite Griffiths had become extremely hostile after his sexual advances were rejected.

The building management became so concerned that it installed closed-circuit cameras and a panic button for its caretaker. An unnamed senior manager with the company that owned the building

was convinced that it was only a matter of time before Griffiths committed murder... which, of course, he did.

It's likely that the true number of women murdered by Stephen Griffiths will never be known. Ultimately, he would admit to just three, the first being 43-year-old Susan Rushworth.

A sex trade worker who struggled with heroin addiction, she was last seen alive near her home during the dying minutes of 22 June 2009. In the months that followed police made numerous appeals to the public, hoping for some hint as to the missing woman's whereabouts.

What the authorities didn't know, but perhaps suspected, was that Susan Rushworth was long dead. It's almost certain that she was killed by Griffiths on the evening of her disappearance.

On April 26 2010, another prostitute, 31-year-old Shelley Armitage, disappeared while working the streets of downtown Bradford. No one noticed at first; two days passed before she was reported missing.

Less than a month later, on 21 May, a Friday, Suzanne Blamires also vanished from the streets of Bradford. The mystery behind the disappearance of this 36-year-old sex trade worker would last only a weekend.

We know that Blamires accompanied Griffiths to his flat, most likely willingly. We also know that she tried to leave. The same security cameras that had

> **Griffiths once appeared in court for leaving threatening messages on the voicemail of a former girlfriend**

been installed in Griffiths' apartment building by concerned management captured her sudden and swift end. Grainy footage shows Blamires fleeing Griffiths' flat with the PhD student in pursuit. He knocks her unconscious, and leaves her lying in the corridor. Moments later, Griffiths returns with a crossbow, aims and shoots a bolt through Blamires' head. Before dragging the woman back into his apartment, he raises his crossbow to the camera in triumph. Moments later, Griffiths returns with a drink, apparently toasting the death. Still later, the murderer can be seen carrying a series of garbage bags out of the building.

The first person to view these images was the building caretaker. He called the police – but not before first selling the story to a tabloid newspaper.

Griffiths was arrested within hours. Asked to confirm his identity, he replied, 'I'm Osama Bin Laden', later adding cryptically, 'I've killed a lot more than Suzanne Blamires – I've killed loads. Peter Sutcliffe [the Yorkshire Ripper] came a cropper in Sheffield. So did I, but at least I got out of the city.'

Authorities searched his home and the immediate area for any sign of Blamires and the other missing women. The small flat was lined with shelves holding hundreds of horror films and books on serial killers, terrorism and genocide. It wasn't strictly true that Griffiths lived alone; he kept two lizards, which he fed baby rats that he bred for just that purpose.

The first body was discovered not by the police,

Crossbows photographed in Griffiths' flat: Suzanne Blamires' head, pierced by a crossbow bolt, was found in a rucksack in the River Aire at Shipley

A forensics officer sifts the area outside Griffiths' home

but by a member of the public in the River Aire. Cut into at least 81 separate pieces, the corpse was not complete. Police divers would recover a black suitcase containing the instruments Griffiths had used to carry out the dissection. As would become clear in the coming days, Griffiths had consumed several pounds of flesh from his victims. The remains would be identified as belonging to Blamires. Identification came without the aid of DNA testing – her head, with the crossbow bolt, was found in a rucksack. At some point Griffiths had embedded a knife in her skull.

The bathtub 'slaughterhouse'

During police interrogations, the man who had rambled continuously on the internet proved oddly reticent. When asked why he felt the need to kill, Griffiths was initially flummoxed. 'I don't know,' he said. But then he added: 'Sometimes you kill someone to kill yourself, or kill a part of yourself. I don't know, I don't know – it's like deep issues inside of me.'

The investigating officer pressed on; 'So, why did you feel the need to kill any of the girls?'

'I don't know,' Griffiths eventually responded. 'I'm

> *The footage showed Armitage naked and bound with the words 'My Sex Slave' spray-painted in black on her back. Griffiths can be heard saying: 'I am Ven Pariah, I am the Bloodbath Artist. Here's a model who is assisting me'*

misanthropic. I don't have very much time for the human race.'

Griffiths gradually opened up about the murders, providing police with macabre details. He described his flat's bathtub as a 'slaughterhouse', saying that it was there that his victims were dismembered. He used power tools on the first two bodies, boiling the parts he ate in a pot.

Blamires was cut up by hand, and her flesh was eaten raw. 'That's part of the magic,' he said, explaining his predilection for human meat.

While Griffiths did not share many details of the actual killings, police had video evidence.

There was, of course, the death of Suzanne Blamires, which had been captured by a security camera, but the horrific images paled next to those of Shelley Armitage.

Griffiths had filmed his second victim's death using his mobile phone, which he subsequently left on a train. The device was bought and sold twice before police managed to track it down. The footage it held was described by one veteran detective as the most disturbing he'd ever viewed.

Armitage is shown naked and bound with the words 'My Sex Slave' spray-painted in black on her back. Griffiths can be heard saying: 'I am Ven Pariah, I am the Bloodbath Artist. Here's a model who is assisting me.'

Only Susan Rushworth was spared the indignity of having her death caught on camera. Investigators believe that she was killed with a hammer.

On 21 December 2010, three days before his 41st birthday, Griffiths pleaded guilty to the murders of Susan Rushworth, Shelley Armitage and Suzanne Blamires.

He was handed down a life sentence. (Bizarrely, he had insisted on being represented by the Bradford law firm Lumb & Macgill, who acted for serial killer Peter Sutcliffe in the early 1980s.)

Since being taken into custody, Griffiths has repeatedly attempted suicide. He also went on a hunger strike, reportedly losing 40 lb (18 kg). Behind bars, Griffiths is less the Crossbow Cannibal, and more the Stickman.

Danger signs: Boyhood cruelty to birds; his obsession with mass murder prompted his choice of studies

----

Pattern of crime: Increasing violence towards women, leading to dismemberment and cannibalism

----

Breakthrough: Closed-circuit television footage showed third murder

----

Behaviour in court: Bold at first appearance, sullen at sentencing

----

Confession: 'I or part of me is responsible for killing Susan Rushworth, Shelley Armitage and Suzanne Blamires, who I know as Amber.'

Sentence: Life without parole

DEATH FARM

Robert Pickton

Name: Robert Pickton

DOB: 25 October 1949

Profession: Farmer

Alias: The Pig Farmer Killer

Previous charges: Attempted murder (dropped), firearms offences

Number of victims: 6 to 49

When Robert Service first cast his eyes on British Columbia, the poet described what he saw as being 'something greater than my imagination had ever conceived'. Canada's westernmost province is known for its natural beauty. Robert Pickton saw these wonders on a daily basis, but his immediate surroundings were much less attractive.

Pickton lived on a pig farm, a muddy, run-down 17-acre parcel of land in Port Coquitlam that he and his siblings had inherited from their parents.

On the occasions that he left his home, Pickton could often be found 30 km (20 miles) away hunting down the drugged and desperate in Vancouver.

For runaways, the homeless and those who were simply down on their luck, British Columbia's biggest city holds an understandable allure.

Nestled by the warm Pacific Ocean, it enjoys a much milder winter than any other major Canadian city. For the drug addict, there's a steady supply of illegal narcotics flowing through its port. For those who still dream of sudden fame, there is fantasy to be found in the city's healthy film industry; 'Hollywood North' is just one of Vancouver's many nicknames.

Sadly, Vancouver is also by far the most expensive city in Canada; in North America it is surpassed only by Manhattan proper. Real estate is at a premium, and rental units are expensive and hard to come by. This city, with the highest concentration of millionaires in North America, is also home to the

Port Coquitlam stands near beautiful countryside. PoCo, as it is known, is Canada's 88th-largest city by population

poorest neighbourhood in the country. Haunted by glorious buildings, reminders of long-gone days as a premier shopping district, Vancouver's Downtown Eastside is a blight on the utopian landscape. The banks disappeared years ago, as did the well-stocked department stores. The few shops that aren't boarded up house lowly pawnbrokers. Outside their doors, and in the blocks that surround, prostitutes – some as young as 11 years old – ply their trade.

Monstrous appetites

Pickton did not prey on children. It's thought that his first victim was a 23-year-old woman named Rebecca Guno, who was last seen on 22 June 1983. She was reported missing three days later – a very short time period compared to the many that followed. The next victim, Sheryl Rail, was not reported missing for three full years. The lives of Guno and Rail were just two of the six Pickton is known to have taken in his first decade of killing. With as much as 28 months separating one murder from the next, the pig farmer had no clear pattern. These early erratic

and seemingly spontaneous killings enabled Pickton to pass under the radar. It wasn't until the closing years of the millennium that speculation began to surface that a serial killer just might be at work on the seedier streets of Vancouver. By then Pickton had picked up the pace; it's believed that he killed nine women in the latter half of 1997 alone.

The next year, the Vancouver Police Department began reviewing cases of missing women stretching back nearly three decades. By this time, talk of a serial killer was a subject of conversation in even the most genteel parts of the city, and still authorities dismissed speculation.

When one of their own, Inspector Kim Rossmo, raised the issue, he was quickly shot down. 'We're in no way saying there is a serial murderer out there,' said fellow inspector Gary Greer. 'We're in no way saying that all these people missing are dead. We're not saying any of that.'

The police posited that the missing women had simply moved on. After all, prostitutes were known to abruptly change locations and even names.

Calgary, 970 km (600 miles) to the east and flush with oil money, was often singled out as a likely destination.

Years later, veteran journalist Stevie Cameron would add this observation: 'There were never any bodies. Police don't like to investigate any case where there isn't a body.'

> ## In 1997, Pickton got into a knife fight with a prostitute on his farm that resulted in both being treated in the same hospital

Even as the authorities dismissed the notion of a serial killer, Pickton continued his bloody work. Among those he butchered was Marcella Creison. Released from prison on 27 December 1998, she never showed at a belated Christmas dinner prepared by her mother and boyfriend. Sadly, 14 days passed before her disappearence was reported.

The waters were muddied by the fact that some of the women who had been reported missing were actually found alive. Patricia Gay Perkins, who had disappeared leaving a 1-year-old son behind, contacted Vancouver Police after reading her name on a list of the missing. One woman was found living in Toronto, while another was discovered to have died of a heroin overdose. However, the list of missing women continued to grow, even as other cases were solved.

Accepting, for a moment, that there was a serial killer on the loose, where were the police to look? There was, it seemed, an embarrassment of suspects – dozens of violent johns who had been rounded up on assault charges during the previous two decades.

However, Robert Pickton was not among them. Should he have been?

In 1997, Pickton got into a knife fight with a prostitute on his farm that resulted in both being treated in the same hospital.

Nurses removed a handcuff from around the woman's wrist using a key that was on Pickton's person. He was charged with attempted murder, though this was later dismissed.

In 1998, Bill Hiscox, one of Pickton's employees, approached police to report on a supposed charity, the Piggy Palace Good Times Society, that was run by Robert and his brother Daniel. Housed in a converted building on the pig farm, Hiscox claimed that it was nothing but a party place populated by a rotating cast of prostitutes.

It wasn't the first police had heard of the Piggy Palace Good Times Society. Established in 1996 to 'co-ordinate, manage and operate special events, functions, dances, shows and exhibitions on behalf of service organizations, sports organizations and other worthy groups', it had continually violated Port Coquitlam city bylaws. There were parties – so many parties – drawing well over 1,000 people to a property that was zoned as agricultural.

The strange goings on at the Piggy Palace Good Times Society might have been a concern, but Hiscox's real focus had to do with the missing women. The Pickton employee told police that purses and other items that could identify the prostitutes would be found on the pig farm.

Police visited the Port Coquitlam property on at least four occasions, once with Hiscox in tow, but found nothing. Robert Pickton would become nothing more than one of many described as 'a person of interest'.

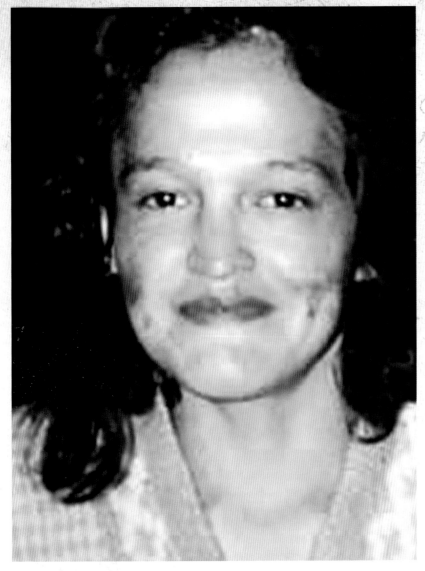

The death of Dawn Crey, 43, was only confirmed when police found her DNA on the farm

Mission to murder

The years passed, women kept disappearing, and still the notion of a serial killer at work in the Downtown Eastside was dismissed.

By 2001, the number of women who had gone missing from the neighbourhood had grown to 65 – a number that police could no longer ignore. That April, a team called 'The Missing Women Task Force' was established. The arrest of Gary Ridgway seven months later by American authorities brought

fleeting interest. Better known as the 'Green River Killer', Ridgway killed scores of prostitutes in the Seattle area, roughly 240 km (150 miles) south of Vancouver. The many murders coincided with the disappearances of the missing women, but it quickly became clear that Ridgway had had nothing to do with events north of the border. The Missing Women Task Force looked into other American serial killers, as well, including foot fetishist Dayton Rogers, 'The Malolla Forest Killer', who had murdered several prostitutes in Oregon.

Despite the newly established task force, prostitutes continued to disappear. No one foresaw the events of February 2002.

Early in the month, Pickton was arrested, imprisoned and charged with a variety of firearms offences, including storing a firearm contrary to regulations, possession of a firearm without a licence and possession of a loaded restricted firearm without a licence. In carrying out the search warrant that led to the charges, police uncovered personal possessions belonging to one of the missing women.

Pickton was released on bail, but was kept under surveillance. On 22 February, he was again taken into custody – this time to be charged with two counts of first-degree murder in the deaths of prostitutes Serena Abotsway and Mona Wilson. The pig farmer would never again experience a day of freedom.

The Pickton farm soon came to look like something out of a science fiction film. Investigators and forensics specialists in contamination suits searched for signs of the missing women. Severed heads were

found in a freezer, a wood chipper contained further fragments, and still more were found in a pigpen and in pig feed. These were easy finds; a team of 52 anthropologists were brought in to do the rest, sifting through 14 acres of soil in search of bones, teeth and hair. Their diligence brought over 10,000 pieces of evidence – and, for Pickton, a further 24 counts of murder.

But to the citizens of Vancouver, particularly the friends and families of the missing women, the breakthrough had come far too late. In place of praise came criticism. How was it that the police had found nothing at all suspicious when they'd visited the farm just a few years earlier? Serena Abotsway, Mona Wilson and several other women whose body parts were found on the farm had disappeared after those initial searches. Might their lives have been spared?

We might add to these questions: What do we now make of Robert Pickton? A decade after he made headlines as Canada's most prolific serial killer, his picture is still coming into focus.

Pickton promised prostitutes not only cash, but drugs and alcohol, if they would only come to Piggy Palace. It's thought that he would almost invariably accuse each of his victims of stealing. He bound

Police went through Pickton's property with a fine-tooth comb – their diligence produced over 10,000 pieces of evidence

each woman, before strangling them with a wire or a belt. Pickton would then drag his victim to the farm's slaughterhouse, where he would use his skills as a butcher.

Some remains he buried on the farm, while others were fed to his pigs. Still more was disposed of at West Coast Reduction Ltd, an 'animal rendering and recycling plant' located well within walking distance of Main and Hastings, the worst corner in the country. In fact, dozens of prostitutes strolled the streets in the shadow of the plant. Eventually, the remains would find their way into cosmetics and animal feed.

Testing found the DNA of some victims in the pork found on the farm. The meat processed on the farm was never sold commercially, though Pickton did distribute it amongst friends and neighbours.

'Nailed to the cross'

It took nearly five years and $100 million to prepare the case against Pickton. The pig farmer denied his guilt to all but one person: a police officer who had been posing as a cellmate. The pig farmer's words were caught by a hidden camera: 'I was gonna do one more, make it an even 50. That's why I was sloppy. I wanted one more. Make... make the big five O.'

Pickton seemed to acknowledge that he was stuck, that there was no way he would be found not guilty. 'I think I'm nailed to the cross,' he told the bogus cellmate. 'But if that happens there will be about 15 other people are gonna go down.'

The statement only added to suspicions that the remains found on the pig farm weren't solely Pickton's work. Yet, on 22 January 2007, when the pig farmer finally had his day in court, he went alone.

The trial proceeded on a group of six counts that had been drawn from the 26 that Pickton faced. As explained by Justice James Williams, the severing had taken place in the belief that a trial dealing with all 26 might take as long as two years to complete, and would place too high a burden on the jury.

As it turned out, Pickton's trial on the six charges lasted nearly 11 months, and was the longest in Canadian history. Pickton, who had pleaded not guilty on all counts, sat barely paying attention as 128 witnesses took the stand.

That he was found guilty came as a surprise to no one, though the details of the verdict were unexpected. On 9 December 2007, after nine long days of deliberation, jurors found Pickton guilty only of six counts of second-degree murder. The men and women were not convinced that Pickton had acted alone.

Robert Pickton was sentenced to life in prison. Though he will be eligible for parole after 25 years, it is unlikely to be granted.

Danger signs: Assault with a knife on a prostitute

Breakthrough: Evidence discovered while carrying out a search for illegal firearms

Behaviour in court: Bored, distracted, given to doodling

Judge's pronouncement: 'Mr Pickton's conduct was murderous and repeatedly so. I cannot know the details but I know this: what happened to them [the women] was senseless and despicable'

Sentence: Life without parole

CONTROL FREAK

Phillip Garrido

Name: Phillip Garrido

DOB: 5 April 1951

Education: High school graduate

Profession: Printer, former drug dealer

Previous convictions: Rape, kidnapping

Accomplice: Nancy Garrido (wife)

Charges: Kidnapping, sexual assault

A baby boomer born within sight of San Francisco, Phillip Garrido was convinced that fame lay in his future. As a young man, he believed that he was destined for stardom as a rock musician. As the years passed, the dream faded and was replaced by the idea of becoming a messianic figure. In the end, he did achieve fame of a kind. However, only one person would ever look up to Phillip Garrido: his wife, the woman who had helped him carry out his despicable crimes.

Phillip Craig Garrido entered the world on 5 April 1951 in Contra Costa County. His father Manuel, a forklift operator, provided a modest, yet comfortable home. Little is known about Phillip's childhood, in part due to the fact that his father demands money in exchange for information about his son.

That said, Phillip's early years may indeed be inconsequential. It may just be that they weren't formative in creating the monster who would become fodder for television newscasts. No, according to some who knew Phillip, his anti-social, dangerous behaviour began with a motorcycle accident he'd suffered as a teenager. On this, even his father was willing to share an opinion. According to Manuel, before the tragic event, Phillip had been a 'good boy'. After? Well, Phillip became uncontrollable and started to take drugs.

Despite his wild behaviour, Phillip graduated from local Liberty High School with the rest of his class. The year was 1969, a time when American counterculture was pervasive. Phillip appeared to

> ## *When his trap was set, Phillip took four tabs of LSD and attacked the woman whom he'd been stalking for so long. Due to his drugged state, she managed to fight him off*

embrace it all. He grew his hair, bought a fringed leather jacket, and played bass in a psychedelic rock group. But in reality, the young high school graduate wanted little to do with peace and love. Eighteen years old, Phillip had already committed his first act of rape, and would regularly beat his girlfriend, Christine Perreira.

In 1972, he was charged with the rape of a 14-year-old girl whom he had plied with barbiturates. Phillip avoided doing time in prison when the girl refused to testify. What the authorities did not realize at the time was that they might have nailed the young man on another charge – Phillip had become one of the busiest drug dealers in Contra Costa County.

Once clear of the rape charge, Phillip married Christine. The young couple settled 300 km (185 miles) northeast in South Lake Tahoe. In the small city, drugs were no longer Phillip's primary source of income. Christine got a job dealing cards at Harrah's Casino, while her husband pursued his dream of becoming a rock star.

Perverted plan

Three years passed, and vinyl glory still eluded Phillip. Each day was blanketed in a haze induced by a combination of marijuana, cocaine and LSD. He would spend hours masturbating while watching elementary school girls across the street, but the real object of his interest was a woman.

Phillip had been following her for months, during which he developed a very elaborate plan, which he set in motion by renting a warehouse in Reno, 100 km (60 miles) to the south. He then fixed up the space, hanging rugs for soundproofing. A mattress was brought in, as were satin sheets, bottles of wine and an extensive collection of pornographic magazines.

When his trap was set, Phillip took four tabs of LSD and attacked the woman whom he'd been stalking for so long. However, due to his drugged state, she managed to fight him off. Frustrated, Phillip drove to Harrah's, where he asked one of his wife's co-workers, Katie Calloway Hall, for a ride home.

Katie was not as lucky as the intended victim. She ended up being raped repeatedly in Phillip's Reno warehouse. After eight hours of pain and humiliation, Katie was rescued by a police officer

Garrido's idea of romance did not involve consent

Garrido and Nancy Bocanegra were married by the prison chaplain at Fort Leavenworth and vouchsafed conjugal visits

whose eye had been drawn to the door, which had been left ajar.

This time, Christine did not stand by Phillip. After her husband's arrest, she severed all ties. The divorce came through just as Phillip was beginning a 50-year

> ### *Carl Probyn watched in horror as his 11-year-old stepdaughter was dragged into a grey sedan. No one was able to supply the licence plate number of the car that sped away*

prison sentence in Leavenworth, Kansas.

However, for Phillip, romance was still in the air. Behind bars he began corresponding with the niece of a fellow inmate, Nancy Bocanegra, four years his junior. In 1981, the two were married in a ceremony that was conducted by the prison chaplain. Phillip was

not yet one tenth of the way through his sentence. When not enjoying conjugal visits with Nancy, he would study psychology and theology. Religion, it seemed, became the focus of his life. A Catholic by birth, he converted, becoming a Jehovah's Witness. Phillip's extreme devotion to the denomination was cited by the prison psychologist as an indication that he would commit no further crimes.

Phillip was granted parole in 1988. With Nancy, he returned to South Lake Tahoe, where they spent nearly three uneventful years.

On 10 June 1991, Phillip's prison psychologist would be proven wrong. That morning, a man named Carl Probyn watched in horror as his 11-year-old stepdaughter was dragged into a grey sedan. He was not alone – several of the girl's friends had also witnessed the abduction – and yet no one was able to provide the licence plate number of the car that sped away.

The girl, Jaycee Dugard, soon found herself living in sheds, tents and under tarpaulins in the backyard of a house in Contra Costa County. The property belonged to Phillip's mother, who was then suffering from dementia. Eventually, the old woman would be shipped off to a chronic care hospital. Jaycee, of course, remained on the property, where she would be subjected to 18 years of sexual abuse at Phillip's hands.

She bore her captor two children, both daughters, born in August of 1994 and November of 1997. Both would come to describe Jaycee as an older sister. It is unknown whether or not they knew the truth.

The girl's nightmare could have ended earlier. Phillip fell under the watchful eyes of his neighbours when it was discovered that he was a registered sex offender.

In 2006, one of the watchful called police to report that Phillip, a 'psychotic sex addict', had a woman and several children living under tents in his backyard. A sheriff's deputy dispatched to investigate interviewed Phillip on his front porch; he did not bother to look at the backyard, nor did he run a background check.

Victim Jaycee Dugard revealed that her kidnappers had told her she had been abducted 'as help for Garrido's sex problem'

Two years later, police were again on Phillip's property, accompanied by firefighters who had been called in to put out a blaze.

Weird and frightening

The actions of law enforcement officers might be considered lazy or negligent, but they paled beside the ineptitude displayed by the California Department of Corrections and Rehabilitation. As a convicted sex offender, Phillip was visited regularly by department employees. All the visits, both scheduled and unscheduled, took place while Jaycee was in the backyard. In nearly two decades, not one department agent would bother investigating Phillip's collection of tents, tarpaulins and sheds.

The authorities might not have thought Phillip was a suspicious character, but those who saw him on a daily basis found him weird and just a little frightening. Neighbourhood parents told their children to keep away from his house. He ran a print shop, Printing for Less, but his behaviour ensured that he had few repeat customers. Those who gave him business would often find themselves subjected to bizarre ramblings. Phillip, the self-proclaimed 'Man Who Spoke with his Mind', would speak of how he could control sound with his mind. Some customers were privileged enough to be shown a machine, through which the printer claimed he could communicate with God. Others might be treated to recordings of songs that Phillip had written about his attraction to underage girls.

Phillip kept a blog, titled 'Voices Revealed', through which he attempted to convince others of his special relationship with God. The outlet seemed to encourage further writing. In August of 2009, he walked into the San Francisco offices of the FBI to hand-deliver two weighty tomes he had

> *Those who gave Garrido business would be subjected to bizarre ramblings. Some customers were privileged to be shown a machine, through which he claimed he could communicate with God. Others might be treated to recordings of songs he had written about his attraction to underage girls...*

written: 'The Origin of Schizophrenia Revealed' and 'Stepping into the Light'. The latter was a personal story in which Phillip detailed how it was that he had come to triumph over his violent sexual urges. Intent on helping others to do the same, he approached Lisa Campbell, a special events coordinator at the University of California, Berkeley, with the idea of a lecture. Phillip was not alone when he made his proposal. Both his daughters sat in on the meeting, listening intently as their father spoke about his deviant past and the rapes he had committed.

It was Campbell's report of the strange behaviour to Phillip's parole officer that at long last brought an end to Jaycee's nightmare.

Moment of truth

When confronted, on 26 August 2009, Phillip admitted to kidnapping Jaycee, adding that he was the father of her children. Both he and Nancy were taken into custody.

On 28 April 2011, Phillip pleaded guilty to Jaycee's

Nancy Garrido pleaded guilty to kidnapping as well as to aiding and abetting a sexual assault.

kidnapping, as well as 13 counts of sexual assault. Sitting next to her husband, Nancy pleaded guilty to the kidnapping, and one charge of aiding and abetting a sexual assault. In court, both Phillip's and Nancy's lawyers portrayed their respective clients as good souls. After 1997, the year in which they both found God, the couple had dedicated themselves to Jaycee and the children – or so the claim went.

Phillip hoped that his confession would win Nancy a lighter sentence. Whether or not he was successful is a matter of debate. What is certain, however, is that Nancy's sentence was not nearly as harsh as that of her husband. Where Phillip received a term amounting to 431 years, Nancy was sentenced to 36 years in prison. Should she live a long life, Nancy Garrido will be 90 when she leaves prison.

Breakthrough: Bizarre behaviour at the University of California, Berkeley

Behaviour in court: Quiet

Plea for the defence: 'It's a disgusting thing that took place with me at the beginning, but I turned my life completely around.'

Victim's statement: 'Phillip Garrido, you are wrong. I could never say that to you before, but I have the freedom now. Everything you have ever done to me has been wrong and some day I hope you can see that.'

Sentence: 431 years

THE POLOGOVSKY MANIAC

Serhiy Tkach

Name: Serhiy Tkach

DOB: 12 September 1952

Profession: Labourer

Aliases: The Pologovsky Maniac

Previous convictions: None (accused of fraud)

Number of victims: 36 to over 100

Short in stature, a quiet man who shied away from eye contact, Serhiy Tkach didn't much look like a murderer, yet for a quarter of a century he took one life after another. It's possible that he was the most prolific serial killer in Ukrainian history. After he was caught, Tkach would happily tell anyone who would listen that his victims numbered over one hundred. This was no confession, but a boast. Tkach was, and remains, proud of the murders he committed.

Serhiy Tkach was born on 12 September 1952 in Kiselyovsk, a Russian city that was then a part of the Soviet Union. By all accounts he did well academically, though he wasn't much interested in higher learning. After fulfilling his compulsory military service, Tkach continued his studies briefly in order to become a police officer. Upon graduation, he became a criminal investigator in Kemerovo, an industrial city in the central Soviet Union. However, what looked to be a long, successful career in law enforcement ended abruptly when Tkach was caught committing fraud. He was only able to avoid prison by writing a letter of resignation.

According to Tkach, he killed for the first time in 1980, not long after his exit in disgrace from the police department. A pleasant, pastoral afternoon, fuelled by numerous bottles of wine, turned horrific when the then 27-year-old grabbed a young woman, dragged her into the bushes and strangled her. Rape, he told one reporter, was his intent; the murder had taken place only because he was fearful

The city of Kemerovo, where Tkach worked as a criminal investigator before embarking on his insane spree of killings

that his victim might somehow escape before he'd completed the assault.

Into the cold

Tkach never identified the woman by name, saying only that she was a former schoolmate whom he had dated on and off for nine years. He added that, in all that time, the two had not had sexual relations. Tkach claimed that on the day of her death, the unnamed woman had slapped his face at the mere suggestion.

'Do you want to know why I killed?' he asked one journalist. 'My main motive was revenge!'

After he returned home, Tkach called the police to report his crime, but was irritated when the officer on the other end of the line refused to identify himself.

'I was going to tell him where to find the corpse,' Tkach told investigators pursuing the case. 'I was going to help my former colleagues, but changed my mind.'

With the loss of his respected position in law enforcement, Tkach became a man adrift. The former criminal investigator worked in mines, on farms and as a low-paid factory worker. He moved from one city to another, leaving a trail of cold bodies in his wake.

Tkach was as meticulous as he was calculating. He was always careful to strip his victims of their jewellery and clothing, some of which he would keep as a trophy. Tkach used his police training in making certain that no fingerprints or traces of semen would be left behind. So as to lend the impression that his murders had occurred far away, he left the bodies close to roads and railways.

It's likely that the most of the murders took place in Ukraine. He killed in the cities of Zaporizhia, Kharkov and, finally, in Dnipropetrovsk, where he lived his final years as a free man.

Ex-policeman Tkach used his specialized knowledge to escape along railway lines treated with tar to throw police dogs off the scent

The vast majority of Tkach's known victims were between 9 and 17 years of age, a fact that has led to doubts about the story of his first killing. His final victim, a 9-year-old identified in the media only as 'Kate', was the daughter of one of Tkach's friends. The girl had been playing with four other children one August 2005 day when she was grabbed. Tkach drowned the girl and, as he had with so very many others, left the body to be found.

Zeroing in on a child whom he had known and carrying out the abduction in front of her friends was uncharacteristically sloppy. Tkach pushed his luck even further by attending the little girl's funeral. He was recognized immediately by her playmates. The former criminal investigator would later express regret that he hadn't bothered to kill them as well.

Tkach was soon dubbed 'The Pologovsky Maniac' after the area of Dnipropetrovsk he had called home. News of his crimes came as a shock to neighbours. Known as a former criminal investigator, the killer had a certain stature within the immediate community. While he was a bit of a loner, and a man of few words, these qualities only added to Tkach's reputation as someone who was highly intelligent. True, Tkach had two failed marriages in his past, but he appeared for all the world to be a devoted husband to wife number three. Unlike so many men in his neighbourhood, he never said a negative word about women. As far as anyone knew, he'd never so much as raised a hand against his wife and four children.

No remorse

More than two years passed before Tkach was put on trial. Much of the delay had to do with the significant challenges that faced investigators.

It wasn't that they had no experience of investigating serial killers – the previous decade, Anatoly Onoprienko, 'The Beast of Ukraine', had been convicted of 52 murders – but with Tkach, the number of victims looked to be much higher. What's more, the Pologovsky Maniac's killing spree had lasted five times longer and stretched to hundreds of kilometres.

There were also legal issues that needed attention. Over the decades, nine innocent men were tried and sentenced for murders that Tkach committed. One of the convicted had committed suicide in prison.

Finally, there were the questions about Tkach's sanity. It beggared belief that anyone in his right mind could commit such horrible acts. Psychiatrists, however, were unanimous in their opinion that Tkach was a sane man. Though he routinely consumed a litre of vodka before each rape and murder, all were convinced that he'd been fully aware of the crimes he had been committing.

> **Twenty-eight years after his first murders, he was able to recall in detail each victim, and the manner in which he'd hunted them down**

Even before the lengthy investigation truly got under way, Tkach began taunting the police. At his arrest, he told officers that he had been expecting them for years, adding that they should have figured things out much sooner.

In interviews with the press Tkach painted those investigating his case as lazy. 'The police couldn't be bothered exhuming bodies,' he said, 'they'd rather I write a letter of confession. I've long laughed at them!'

When it finally began, the trial lasted almost all of 2008.

Speaking from a cage within the courtroom, Tkach demonstrated that the memories of his victims remained fresh in his mind. Twenty-eight years after his first murders, he was able to recall in detail each victim, and the manner in which he'd hunted them down.

Tkach expressed no remorse – not for his victims, not for the wrongly accused. He defended his actions with the claim that the killings had been committed for no other reason than to expose the police as a group of bumbling incompetents. Yet, he would also describe himself frequently as a beast, a creature who not only deserved, but desired the death penalty.

Ultimately, Tkach would be disappointed in his wish for a quick end to his life. Ukraine having abolished capital punishment, Tkach was sentenced to life in prison for the murders of 36 of the more than one hundred girls and women that he claimed to have deprived of life. 'No one has been able to determine the motives for his actions,' declared Judge Serhiy Voloshko after delivering his verdict.

Christmas Day 2008 marked the first full day of his sentence, but to Tkach the date meant nothing. 'I do not believe in God or the Devil,' he'd declared. Perhaps not, but to many his actions were clear evidence of the existence of the latter.

Pattern of crime: Meticulous in removing evidence from bodies

Breakthrough: Recognized at the funeral of his final victim

Behaviour in court: Defiant

Statement of defence: 'I took revenge on the cops, because they do not work – they never work!'

Sentence: Life without parole

THE WESTSIDE RAPIST

John Thomas, Jr

Name: John Thomas, Jr

DOB: 26 June 1936

Profession: Insurance claims adjuster

Alias: The Westside Rapist

Previous convictions: Rape, attempted rape, burglary

Number of victims: 7 to 30

He too would torture, rape and kill, but unlike the men behind the Hillside Strangler murders, his crimes did not end with an arrest. In 1978, the Westside Rapist seemed to vanish. Authorities came to believe that the man responsible for the crimes had either died or was incarcerated.

Little boy lost

More than three decades passed, during which the name and associated crimes began to fade from public consciousness. Then, on 31 March 2009, the words 'Westside Rapist' made a sudden and unexpected return to the headlines with the arrest of John Floyd Thomas, Jr, a friendly 72-year-old insurance claims adjuster.

Thomas was living in Los Angeles, as he had nearly all his life. He was born in the city on 26 June 1936. The son of an absentee father, there was little in his early life that was enviable. Not even the death

With the Black Dahlia Murder, the Manson Murders and the butchering of Nicole Brown and Ron Goldman, Los Angeles has been the site of many of the 20th century's most bloody and bizarre homicides. The city has also been home to several serial killers, including 'The Hillside Strangler' – in actuality two cousins – who in the 1970s terrorized residents by torturing, raping and killing a total of 12 girls and women. Their crimes overlapped those of another serial killer, a mysterious figure who for decades was known only as 'The Westside Rapist'.

of his mother, when he was just 12, could bring back the man after whom he had been named. Instead, Thomas was shuttled between an aunt and a godmother. A middling student, he managed to graduate from high school, and in 1956 enlisted in the United States Air Force.

Thomas ended up being stationed at Nellis Air Force Base, just outside Las Vegas, Nevada. A little over 400 km (250 miles) from home, it would be the farthest he would ever get from Los Angeles.

During Thomas' very brief time as a serviceman, he proved himself to be anything but air force material. In 1957, the year

Thomas joined the air force and was stationed at Nellis Air Force Base, Nevada

after he enlisted, the Los Angeleno received a dishonourable discharge.

The dismissal had nothing to do with the contents of his file – Thomas was often criticized for being 'slovenly' and perpetually late – but for a burglary and attempted rape he had committed in his home town. At the age of 21, Thomas entered the penal system for what should have been a six-year sentence. However, with bad behaviour and two

> **Within just a few years, Thomas would embark upon a trail that would lead him to become the most prolific serial killer in the history of Los Angeles**

parole violations, it was 1966 before he was finally clear of prison.

Now 30 and finally a free man, Thomas entered the workforce for the first time. He held a variety of jobs, including hospital employee, electronics salesman and, incredibly, social worker.

Within just a few years, Thomas would embark upon a trail that would lead him to become the most prolific serial killer in the history of Los Angeles. A black man, he preyed exclusively on white women aged from 50 to 90. More often than not his victims were widows who lived alone. Like other serial killers, he developed a routine. Thomas would begin with rape, before using his bare hands in an attempt to literally squeeze the life from each victim. Once finished, he usually covered the face of his victim with a blanket or pillow. It would appear that Thomas did not realize that some of the women did not die, but had passed out from lack of oxygen. At least 20 women survived his assaults, although none of them could identify their assailant.

Like the Hillside Strangler, the Westside Rapist was a focus of police attention. A special investigative unit was dedicated to catching the murderer. Concerted efforts were made to inform the public of the danger, and still the rapes and murders continued.

The reign of terror attributed to the Westside Rapist ended in 1978, when Thomas was tried and convicted – tellingly – of rape. He was only caught after alert neighbours of the victim noted the licence plate on his car as he sped away from the scene of the crime. Thomas was sentenced to five years in prison. Upon his release, he committed at least five more sexual assaults and murders of elderly women in nearby Claremont, all the while working as a hospital counsellor.

Curiously, despite all the resources that had been allocated to the capture of the Westside Rapist – and the obvious similarities – the Los Angeles Police Department never linked the two sets of crimes.

Unlike the first, the second sequence of rape and murder appeared to end of Thomas' own volition. After 1988, there is no evidence that he was guilty of so much as jaywalking in the 20 years before he was apprehended.

Thomas might have escaped justice completely had it not been for advances in DNA research. Taking advantage of growing state and federal DNA databases, in 2001 the Los Angeles Police Department created a special Cold Case Homicide Unit. It focused exclusively on murders that had been committed in the city during the previous four decades, including the once high-profile Westside Rapist murders.

Elizabeth McKeown, 67, was murdered by Thomas in the Westchester area

It took time but the LAPD's Cold Case Homicide Unit finally got their man

> ***Thomas had raped, beaten and strangled the twice-widowed 80-year-old grandmother just minutes after she'd returned home from church choir practice***

Thomas never stood trial for his crimes. On 2 April 2011, as part of a deal struck to avoid the death penalty, he pleaded guilty to the sexual assault and murder of all seven women. The Westside Rapist received seven life sentences without the chance of parole. He remains a suspect in 15 other murders.

Maybelle Hudson's nephew, Bob Kistner, himself a police officer, spoke out on Thomas. 'I know my aunt, the very good Christian that she was, would be hoping for the salvation of his soul and looking for forgiveness. I come from the law enforcement side of it – I can't be quite as forgiving, I'm afraid.'

Unforgiven

Thomas' DNA was not entered into the database until seven years later, when he was ordered to provide samples as part of an ongoing effort to catalogue all registered sex offenders.

The first match investigators discovered linked Thomas to Ethel Sokoloff and Elizabeth McKeown, both of whom had been raped and murdered in the 1970s. Others were quick to follow. As he awaited trial, five more rape and murder charges were added, including that of a gentle, pious lady named Maybelle Hudson.

In April 1976, Thomas had raped, beaten and strangled the twice-widowed 80-year-old grandmother just minutes after she'd returned home from church choir practice.

Pattern of crime: Victims invariably middle-aged or elderly white women living alone

Breakthrough: DNA sample collected

Behaviour in court: Impassive

Victim impact statement: 'She was beloved – her life mattered to many people – and this man came along and stalked her and preyed upon her.' Tracey Michaels, great-niece of Elizabeth McKeown

Sentence: Seven consecutive life sentences without parole

THE SHOE FETISH SLAYER

Jerry Brudos

Name: Jerry Brudos

DOB: 31 January 1939

Profession: Electronics technician

Category: Brudos was diagnosed schizophrenic and spent his teenage years in and out of mental hospital

Previous convictions: At the age of 17, he was sent to the Oregon State Hospital psychiatric ward after confessing to holding a girl at knife-point in a hole he dug to imprison 'sex slaves'

Number of victims: 4

For most of his 67 years, Jerome Henry Brudos was simply called 'Jerry', but he would become famous as 'The Shoe Fetish Slayer' and 'The Lust Killer'. Neither appellation quite covers what he was – for one, his fetishes went way beyond footwear. What is more, both nicknames suggest that Jerry's crimes extended no further than murder when in fact he was a torturer and a rapist, with an attraction toward necrophilia.

Brudos was born on 31 January 1939, in the small South Dakota town of Webster. Times were hard for his family. They had suffered under the weight of the Great Depression for nearly a decade. Not long after welcoming the new baby, they gave up on their farm and moved to Oregon, but the move did not bring the financial stability they had hoped for. Jerry's father, Henry, was forced to work at two jobs and he had little time to spend with the family.

When he was not at school, Jerry was usually with his domineering, stern mother, Eileen. It's strange that this is so – Eileen didn't like Jerry. She much preferred her eldest son, Larry, on whom she constantly doted.

Her resentment of Jerry can be traced back to his birth. As the mother of three sons she had desperately wanted her fourth child to be a girl, but

One of the homes where Brudos was brought up – the family had moved up in the world but he still felt a disappointment to his mother

Jerry had arrived instead. He grew up feeling that his mother was not happy about his gender.

Eileen's disappointment with Jerry's sex might explain a rather curious incident from his early life. At the age of 5, he found a pair of elegant women's high-heeled shoes at the local dump. He began wearing them in secret around the house, but his mother soon saw what he was doing. She flew into a rage and then she insisted that he get rid of the feminine footwear. When she discovered that Jerry had not done as she requested, she doused the offending items in petrol and set them alight. Then she forced Jerry to watch as the forbidden footwear went up in flames.

Whatever Eileen's intention, it is likely that she only intensified her son's interest in women's footwear. In short, it was the attraction to the forbidden. Not long afterwards, Jerry was caught trying to steal his nursery school teacher's shoes.

By 1955 the Great Depression and the hardship it had caused seemed far away. The Brudos family had moved into an attractive middle-class home in a pleasant neighbourhood.

Now 16 years old, Jerry found himself living next door to a couple with three teenage daughters. He not only spied on the girls from the windows of his home, but he began stealing their underwear from the clothes line.

After the theft of the missing articles had been reported to the police, Jerry saw an opportunity to further his increasingly unusual desire for things feminine. He began by convincing one of the girls that he was working on the crime with the police and then he invited her over to discuss the case. When the girl appeared, Jerry invited her in and then he excused himself and left the room. He returned wearing a mask. Suddenly he held a knife to her throat and forced her to strip.

Once her clothes were on the floor, Jerry took a number of photographs before leaving the room. He reappeared just as his neighbour was about to flee. Before she could raise the alarm, he quickly explained that a masked man had locked him up. It was a bold story, a ridiculous story, yet the girl told no one about the bizarre and terrifying experience.

Unhealthy fantasies

Not long afterwards an emboldened Jerry began beating another girl after she had refused to strip for him, but he was interrupted by an elderly couple who happened to be out for a stroll. The police were called, a report was made and an investigation began. They soon found Jerry's shoe collection, the stolen lingerie and the nude photographs he had taken of his neighbour.

> *Jerry began beating a girl who had refused to strip for him. The police were called... and they found his shoe collection, stolen lingerie and nude photographs*

Jerry was sent to the psychiatric ward at Oregon State Hospital, where he related his fantasies to the psychiatrists. One of them involved an underground prison. He dreamt of a place in which he could keep captured girls. That way, he would be able to have any girl he wanted, whenever he wanted.

The psychiatrists were not concerned by what they were hearing, because they believed that Jerry's dark sexual desires would pass with adolescence. The same psychiatrists determined that Jerry was

borderline schizophrenic, yet after nine months at the hospital he was discharged. Tests revealed that Jerry was an intelligent person, yet he lacked motivation and self-discipline. When he graduated from high school he ended up very close to the bottom of his class.

Jerry gave no thought to university. Instead he looked for a job, but he found nothing.

Unusual requests

Having come to a dead end, he set his sights on a military career, but he was soon discharged as an undesirable recruit after sharing his sexual fantasies with an army psychiatrist. Forced to return home, he lapsed into his old habits. He not only began stealing shoes and underwear but he also went back to assaulting women. Taking things a stage further he tried to abduct one young woman, but when she lost consciousness Jerry stole her shoes instead.

By 1961 Jerry had become an electronics technician. While he was working at a local radio station he took up with an attractive girl named Ralphene. The 17-year-old liked the idea of dating a man who was five years her senior. At the age of 23, Jerry finally lost his virginity. It was not long before Ralphene became pregnant, so with considerable reluctance her parents agreed to a wedding.

The ceremony took place in the spring of 1962, but there was not much of a honeymoon. Ralphene soon discovered that her new husband was very controlling.

What is more, his requests were really peculiar. Jerry insisted that his bride do all her housework in the nude… except for a pair of high-heeled shoes, of course. Jerry also forbade Ralphene to enter his basement. Unbeknown to his wife, Jerry spent his time printing photographs of Ralphene wearing the articles

Jerry turned inwards. He began wearing his collection of stolen women's underwear on a daily basis, often under his work clothes.

Things escalated dramatically one evening, shortly after the birth of his second child. Quite by chance Jerry spotted a very attractive woman walking down a street in Portland. He followed her to her apartment and then he stood and watched her windows. The hours went by, but Jerry did not move until he was certain that she had gone to sleep. He then broke in. The woman woke up just as he was in the process of stealing her underwear, so he jumped on the bed and raped her.

Frustrated by Ralphene's refusal to participate in his fantasies, Jerry took photographs of himself in women's clothing and then he left them around the house. When they were ignored, he retreated into his basement workshop. Jerry had already committed rape, but his sexual fantasies were about to manifest themselves in an even more violent fashion.

On 26 January 1968 he committed his first murder. His victim, 19-year-old Linda Slawson, was trying to fund her education as a door-to-door encyclopedia saleswoman.

When she approached Jerry in his garden he expressed great enthusiasm, so she willingly followed him into his basement so that she could continue her sales pitch. Once inside, she was clubbed on the head and strangled.

When he was certain that Linda was dead, he went upstairs, peeled some bills from his wallet and sent his family out to a local fast food restaurant. Once they had left, he began acting out his fantasies

Linda Slawson was trying to fund her education by selling encyclopedias door to door

of women's clothing that he had stolen over the years.

Ralphene was young and inexperienced when the couple were first married, so she went along with her husband's unusual requests, but as time went on she became more assertive. No longer was Jerry's wife willing to be photographed, no longer would she don the underwear he gave her. The housework was now done in an overall. She was a mother now, with another child on the way. Now that Ralphene was no longer an outlet for his sexual fantasies, with the dead woman's body. But Jerry did not stop when his wife and children returned – in fact, he continued with his activities for several days.

He then dipped into his collection of shoes and women's underwear so that he could dress Linda's body in high heels and lingerie. Numerous photographs were taken, the articles of clothing would be changed and the cycle would be repeated. Jerry also had sex with Linda's body. After a few days of exhausting activity he took the corpse to the Willamette River and threw it from a bridge. Before doing so, he cut off one of Linda's feet with a hacksaw and placed it in the basement freezer. From time to time, Jerry would place a shoe on the severed foot and then masturbate. When the severed foot had almost rotted away, Brudos threw it into the river to join the corpse.

Jerry did not kill again for several months. In the intervening period he moved his family to Salem, Oregon's state capital. The new Brudos home was rather unattractive, but it did have one feature that appealed to the head of the household – a separate garage. Located off a narrow roadway, the structure would serve as Jerry's new workshop. It would be much more private than the basement.

Hung from a meat hook

On the evening of 26 November 1968 Jerry abducted Jan Whitney, his second murder victim. The family had not even settled in at that point. He had come across the young woman on Interstate 5 (I-5), after spotting her broken-down car. The vehicle could be fixed, or so he claimed, but first he had to return to his home to retrieve some tools. Jan went back to Salem with Jerry. Once there, Jerry raped and strangled her in the passenger seat of the family car.

During the next five days, Jan's body hung from a meat hook in Jerry's garage. He dressed the corpse, took photographs and committed acts of necrophilia, as before. Then he took a break by going off on a Thanksgiving weekend getaway with his wife and family.

While the Brudos family were away a freak accident very nearly exposed Jan's dangling corpse and with it Jerry's secret life. A car spun out of control and hit his garage with such force that it made a large crack in the wooden structure, which brought several police officers to the scene. Had they bothered to look through the damaged wall they would have seen Jan Whitney's hanging body.

The close call served to embolden Jerry. He thought he was so clever that he could do whatever he pleased without being caught. A few days after his return, Jerry disposed of Jan's corpse in the Willamette River. Before doing so he cut off her right breast, intending to use it as a mould for making paperweights. He would be frustrated in his attempts.

> *Dressed in women's clothing, he hung around in a Salem department store parking garage and on 27 March he abducted his next victim, 19-year-old Karen Sprinker*

Linda Slawson's work had led her to approach Jerry, while Jan Whitney's murder was the result of a chance encounter – now, however, Jerry was ready to stalk his prey. Dressed in women's clothing, he hung around in a Salem department store parking garage and on 27 March 1969 he abducted his next

The Willamette River where Brudos dumped the bodies of Linda Slawson and Jan Whitney

victim. Jerry did not kill 19-year-old Karen Sprinker immediately. Instead he forced her to model various items from his collection of women's clothing. After he became tired of that game, he put a noose around her neck, raised her a few inches above the ground and left his garage workshop to join his family for dinner. When he returned, Karen was dead. He cut off both of her breasts in yet another attempt at making a paperweight and then he threw her into the Long Tom River.

Less than a month later, Jerry was hunting for a new victim. On 21 April he attacked another young woman, Sharon Wood, in a parking garage. A struggle ensued, Sharon bit Jerry's thumb and he ran. A few days later he tried again, this time choosing a much younger target. As 12-year-old Gloria Smith walked to school, he approached her with a fake pistol and began marching her to his car. Fortunately Gloria showed quick thinking by running to a woman who was working in her garden.

Fake police badge

Jerry had thought himself so clever, but he had now failed on two occasions. He had even been outwitted by a young girl. Clearly he needed more than an imitation pistol if his abductions were going to be successful. So Jerry went out and bought a fake police badge, which he used to abduct Linda Salee, his final victim. He approached the young woman in a Portland shopping centre car park and accused her of shoplifting. After meekly following his orders, Linda was driven back to his Salem garage where she was tied up. Jerry then had dinner in the house with his family. On his return, he was surprised to find that Linda had removed the ropes. The young woman was free and yet she had not fled, so Jerry tied her up a second time and suspended her from the ceiling. After undressing her and taking a series of photographs, he hanged her.

Linda was Jerry's fourth murder victim and yet the police had not linked the murders together. In fact,

Jerry Brudos is marched into court by police officers – when he was arrested, he was wearing women's underwear

they did not even know that the women were dead. Jerry might have gone on killing for some time had it not been for an angler's discovery.

On 10 May 1969, roughly a month after Linda's murder, the man spotted her body floating in the Long Tom River. Two days later, police divers found Karen Sprinker's remains. They were just a few feet away from Linda's corpse.

Jerry was unconcerned when the news raced through the community. He was confident that nothing could link him to the bodies.

He was wrong.

When Jerry had tied the women up he had used an unusual knot, one that was often used by electricians when they pulled wires through a house. The knot would tie Jerry to the murders.

The police then visited the campus of Oregon State University, where Karen Sprinker had been a student. They were told stories about a peculiar man who had been seen roaming the campus. One young woman had even had a date with the man.

When he called again, the police were waiting. It was Jerry Brudos. A background check revealed Jerry's occupation and his history of attacking teenage girls, so detectives paid a visit to the Brudos home.

They noticed a piece of rope in Jerry's garage. It was identical to the one that had been tied around the two bodies that had been found in the Long Tom River. Recognizing the investigators' interest, the ever-bold Jerry offered them a sample. It later proved to be a perfect match.

The net tightens

Jerry could sense that the police were closing in, so on 30 May he made for the Canadian border, accompanied by his wife. The couple were spotted by the Oregon State Police. Although Jerry was arrested on the relatively minor charge of armed assault in relation to 12-year-old Gloria Smith, he became talkative in custody. He took great pleasure in providing very detailed accounts of the murders that he had committed. At the same time he showed no remorse, telling one detective that the women he had abused and killed were nothing more than objects to him. In fact, he went so far as to compare each of the dead women to a candy wrapper.

'Once you're done with them, you just discard them. Why would you not discard them? You don't have any more use for them.'

On 27 June, Jerry pleaded guilty to all of the charges that had been made against him. He received three life sentences amounting to at least 36 years in prison. Jerry became eligible for parole in 2005, but as the years passed and the date of his release approached it became increasingly clear that he would never again be a free man.

He died of liver cancer on 29 March 2006, at the age of 67.

Danger signs: Found women's shoe catalogues arousing; made his wife wander naked round the house; wore women's underwear

Pattern of crime: Stalked women as a teenager, assaulting them and stealing their shoes; became more and more calculating and violent

Breakthrough: The police found photographs of his victims posed in his underwear collection; body parts were stored in his home

Sentence: The death penalty (but he died of natural causes)

THE LURKING COMMUNIST

Andrei Chikatilo

Name: Andrei Chikatilo

DOB: 16 October 1936

Profession: Employee of shipping firm

Upbringing: Born at a time of famine; told that his brother had been eaten by ravenous neighbours; chronic bed-wetter

Description: His head was misshapen from water on the brain as a child; called himself 'a mistake of nature'

Previous convictions: Career as a teacher was blighted by accusations he had molested pupils of both sexes

Number of victims: 52 at least

Even as the USSR retreats into history, there is something almost surreal in the grouping of the words 'Soviet serial killer'. Rightly or wrongly, the phenomenon often seems so much a symptom of the West. How incredible, then, that a serial killer from the Soviet Union was more prolific and, one might claim, more sadistic than any of his Western contemporaries. Andrei Chikatilo is thought to have raped and killed at least 52 people of both sexes. He mutilated their bodies, often in ways reminiscent of Jack the Ripper.

Andrei Romanovich Chikatilo was born on 16 October 1936 in Yablochnoye, a village in what is now Ukraine. As a child he suffered terribly, growing up with the after-effects of the Ukrainian famine. His mother often told him a story that he'd had an older brother, Stepan, who had been kidnapped and then consumed by starving neighbours.

No documentary evidence supports the existence of this sibling.

After the Soviet Union entered the Second World War, when he was 4, his father went off to fight. Chikatilo was left alone with his mother, sharing her bed each night. A chronic bed-wetter, he was beaten for each offence. As the war progressed, he was witness to the Nazi occupation and the massive devastation and death caused by German bombing

Chikatilo was born in the aftermath of the Ukrainian famine of the 1930s

raids. Dead bodies, not an uncommon sight, were things he found both frightening and exciting.

The end of the war brought little happiness to the Chikatilo household. His father, who had spent much of the conflict as a prisoner of war, was transferred to a Russian prison camp.

Outsider

Awkward and overly-sensitive, Chikatilo withdrew from other children. He was considered a good student, but failed his entrance exam to Moscow State University. In 1960, after finishing his compulsory military service, he found work as a telephone engineer. It was during this period that Chikatilo, now 23 years old, attempted his first relationship with a woman. He found himself unable to perform sexually, a humiliation

> **Now 23 years old, Chikatilo attempted his first relationship with a woman. He found himself unable to perform sexually...**

that his prospective girlfriend spread among his acquaintances. As a result, he developed elaborate fantasies of revenge in which he would capture the woman and tear her apart.

When Chikatilo married, in 1963, it was through the work of his younger sister, who made the arrangement with one of her friends. He suffered from chronic impotence, yet managed to father a son and daughter.

Late in life it was discovered that he had suffered brain damage at birth, which affected his ability to control his bladder and seminal emissions.

In 1971, after completing a degree in Russian literature through a correspondence course, he managed to get a teaching position at a local school. Though a poor instructor, Chikatilo continued in the profession for nearly a decade, often dodging accusations that he had molested his students.

In 1978, having accepted a new teaching position, Chikatilo moved to Shakhty. Living alone, waiting until his family could join him, he began to fantasize about naked children. Chikatilo bought a hut off a shabby side street from which he would spy on children as they played, all the while indulging in his solitary practices. Three days before Christmas, he managed to lure a 9-year-old girl, Yelena Zabotnova, into his lair. He had intended to rape the girl, but found himself unable to achieve an erection. He then grabbed a knife and began stabbing her, ejaculating in the process. He later disposed of the girl's body by dumping it into the Grushovka River. Chikatilo was a suspect in the crime; several witnesses had seen him with the girl and blood was discovered on his doorstep. However, another man, Alexsandr Kravchenko, confessed to the murder under torture. Kravchenko was subsequently executed.

In a world where censorship ruled, rumours rapidly spread that a werewolf was the killer

Chikatilo most often preyed on runaways and prostitutes who he found at railway and bus stations. Enticing his victims with the promise of cigarettes, alcohol, videos or money, he would lead them into nearby forests. The corpse of one young female runaway, discovered in 1981, is typical of the horrific scenes Chikatilo would leave behind. Covered by a newspaper, she was lacking her sexual organs. One breast was left bloody by a missing nipple. Chikatilo later admitted that he had bitten and swallowed it, an act which caused him to ejaculate involuntarily.

His male victims, all of whom ranged in age from 8 to 16, were treated in a different manner. It was Chikatilo's fantasy that each was being held prisoner for some undisclosed crime.

He would torture them, all the while fantasizing that he was a hero for doing so. Chikatilo would offer no explanation as to why, more often than not, he would remove the penis and tongue while his victim was still alive.

Many of his early victims had their eyes cut out, an act performed in the belief that they would provide a snapshot of his face. The practice all but stopped when, upon investigation, Chikatilo realized this to be an old wives' tale.

Chikatilo's good luck did not transfer to his new school. In 1981, he was dismissed after molesting boys in the school dormitory. Through his membership of the Communist party, he was soon given a position as a supply clerk at a nearby factory.

Though he did not kill again until the 3 September 1981 murder of Larisa Tkachenko, Chikatilo had begun a series of murders that lasted until the month of his capture, 12 years later.

There can be little doubt that Chikatilo was greatly aided in his crimes by the state-controlled media of his time. No-one knew what was going on. Reports of crimes like rape and serial murder were uncommon, and seemed invariably to be associated

Police photographs of Chikatilo carrying the black bag which contained the knives used on his victims

with what was portrayed as the hedonistic West.

While close to 600 detectives and police officers worked on the case, staking out bus and train stations, and interrogating suspects, those living in the areas where the bodies were found were entirely unaware that there might be a serial killer in their midst. Still, with over half a million people having been investigated, there were bound to be rumours.

One story had it that boys and girls were being mauled by a werewolf. It was not until August 1984, after Chikatilo had committed his 30th murder, that the first news story was printed in the local party daily.

Suspicious behaviour

On 14 September 1984, there was a break in the case when an undercover officer spotted Chikatilo approaching various young women at the Rostov bus station. When questioned, Chikatilo explained that, as a former schoolteacher, he missed speaking

> *There was a break in the case when an undercover officer spotted Chikatilo approaching young women at Rostov bus station*

with young people. The explanation did nothing to allay suspicions and the officer continued to trail Chikatilo. Eventually, the former teacher approached a prostitute and, after having received oral sex, was picked up by the police. His briefcase, when searched, was found to contain a kitchen knife, a towel, a rope and a jar of petroleum jelly.

So certain were the authorities that they had their serial killer that the prosecutor was asked to come and interrogate Chikatilo. However, any celebration was cut short when it was discovered that Chikatilo's blood type did not match that of the semen found on the victims' bodies. This discrepancy, which has never been satisfactorily explained, is most often considered the result of a clerical error. After two days, Chikatilo was released, having admitted to nothing more than soliciting a prostitute.

There is the possibility that Chikatilo would have remained under interrogation for a longer period had it not been for the fact that he was a member of the Communist party.

This association would quickly come to an end weeks after his near-capture when he was arrested and charged with petty theft from his workplace. Chikatilo was expelled by the party and sentenced to three months in prison.

After his release, Chikatilo found new work in Novocherkassk. His killing began again in August 1985 and remained irregular for several years. By 1988, however, he seemed to have returned to his old ways, murdering at least nine people.

And yet it appears he took no life during the calendar year that followed. In 1990, he killed nine more people, the last being on 6 November, when he mutilated Sveta Korostik in the woods near the Leskhoz train station.

With the station under constant surveillance, Chikatilo was stopped and questioned as he emerged from the area

The body of Tanya Petrosan, 32, who was murdered in 1984

> **Within the next 15 days, he confessed to and described 56 murders. The number shocked the police, who had counted just 36 killings during their investigation**

where the body would later be discovered.

On 14 November, the day after Sveta Korostik's body was discovered, Chikatilo was arrested and interrogated. Within the next 15 days, he confessed to and described 56 murders. The number shocked the police, who had counted just 36 killings during their investigation.

Crazy outbursts

Chikatilo finally went to trial on 14 April 1992. Manacled, he was placed in a large iron cage in the middle of the courtroom. It had been constructed specially for the trial, primarily to protect him from the families of his victims. As the trial got under way, the mood of the accused alternated between boredom and outrage. On two occasions Chikatilo exposed himself, shouting out that he was not a homosexual.

Chikatilo's testimony was equally erratic. He denied having committed several murders to which he'd already confessed, while admitting his guilt in others which were unknown. Claiming other murders as his own seemed less bizarre than other statements. At various points Chikatilo announced that he was pregnant, that he was lactating and that he was being radiated. On the day the prosecutor was to give his closing argument, Chikatilo broke into song and had to

be removed from the courtroom. When he was brought back and offered a final opportunity to speak, he remained mute.

On 14 October 1992, six months after his trial had begun, Chikatilo was found guilty of murdering 21 males and 31 females. All of the males and 14 of the females had been under the age of 18.

Throughout the trial, Chikatilo's lawyer had made repeated attempts to prove that his client was insane, but a panel of court-appointed psychiatrists dismissed the claim. An appeal having been rejected, on St Valentine's Day, 1994, Chikatilo was taken to a special soundproof room and executed with a single gunshot behind his right ear.

Danger signs: As a young teacher he spent his free time watching children, picturing them naked

Pattern of crime: Impotence exacerbated his feelings of inadequacy; found he could only achieve an erection while stabbing and slashing victims

Breakthrough: Observed by undercover policeman trying to lure young women from Rostov bus station

Behaviour in court: Exposed himself in court, crying out he was not homosexual; broke into song and refused to answer questions

Plea for the defence: 'I considered them [his victims] enemy aircraft to be shot down'

Sentence: Death (gunshot to the head in a soundproofed room)

BEAST IN THE BUNKER

Josef Fritzl

Name: Josef Fritzl

DOB: 9 April 1935

Profession: Technical equipment salesman and landlord

Upbringing: Claimed his mother hit him until he was covered in blood

Previous conviction: Sentenced to 18 months in jail for rape

Charges: False imprisonment, rape, incest, coercion, enslavement and negligent homicide

Josef Fritzl told conflicting stories about his mother Maria. In some, she was 'the best woman in the world', in others she had been a cold, brutal being – almost inhuman. 'She used to beat me, hit me until I was lying in a pool of blood on the floor,' he once claimed. 'I never had a kiss from her.'

Later on, Fritzl claimed, his mother did not mellow with age. Instead, her harsh nature stayed with her, even into old age. When Fritzl was a senior citizen himself, he revealed that Maria's last years were spent in a locked room with a bricked-up window. Fritzl told concerned neighbours that his mother had died, when in reality she had been his captive. In ordinary circumstances, Fritzl's behaviour towards his mother would be shocking, but in the context of his other crimes the incident ranks as little more than a footnote.

Deathly pale

The world knew nothing of Fritzl's crimes until the morning of Saturday 19 April 2008, when he telephoned for an ambulance. Seventeen-year-old Kerstin Fritzl was seriously ill at his home, number 40 Ybbsstrasse in the Austrian town of Amstetten.

The ambulance attendants were puzzled by the condition of their unconscious patient. Her symptoms were like nothing they had ever encountered. Deathly pale and missing many of her teeth, Kerstin was close to death. She was transported immediately

Fritzl explained Elisabeth's disappearance by saying she had joined a cult

to the local hospital. A few hours later, Josef Fritzl turned up. Describing himself as her grandfather, he presented a letter from Kerstin's mother, Elisabeth.

Please help her. Kerstin is very scared of strangers. She has never been in a hospital before. I've asked my father for help because he is the only person she knows.

Josef Fritzl explained Elisabeth had run off to join a religious cult many years before, leaving the child with him. The police were called in as Kerstin lay close to death and a team of investigators began a search for Elisabeth Fritzl. The authorities wanted to question the mother about what they thought might be criminal neglect. Enquiries were made all over Austria and all sorts of databases were checked, yet nothing could be found on Elisabeth that was not at least a few decades old.

Televised appeal

At the end of Kerstin's second day in hospital, the doctors made a televised appeal. They were struggling to diagnose Kerstin's condition and they thought that her mother might be able to help them. When Elisabeth failed to contact the hospital the police showed up at 40 Ybbsstrasse. They wanted to take DNA samples from the Fritzls. Josef's wife Rosemarie provided a sample, as did the other children that Elisabeth had previously abandoned. However, Josef himself was far too busy to give the authorities even a few minutes of his time.

One week after Kerstin had been taken to hospital, Rosemarie was surprised to see Elisabeth in her house. Her daughter had been away for nearly 24 years. Elisabeth was accompanied by two children, Stefan and Felix. Rosemarie had not been aware of their existence. Josef explained that their daughter had heard the doctors' appeals and had left the cult she had been with, so that she could see her seriously ill daughter.

When Elisabeth visited the hospital, the police were waiting. They wanted to know where the young woman had been during the previous two decades, and how it was that she had abandoned her children. Elisabeth was taken to the police station, where she was questioned for hours. As midnight approached, Elisabeth revealed that she had not joined a cult and she had not abandoned her children. Instead, she had been imprisoned by her father in the cellar at 40 Ybbsstrasse.

Having broken her silence, Elisabeth told the police that she would reveal everything about the last 24 years of her life on condition that she never had to see her father again.

After the stunned investigators had acceded to her wishes, Elisabeth began a two-hour monologue in which she described in considerable detail the ordeal she had endured.

She told the police that her father had lured her

into the cellar on 29 August 1984, where she had been sedated with ether and placed in a hidden bunker.

It seemed that the foundations of number 40 Ybbsstrasse were something of a maze. The oldest part of the house dated back to 1890 and numerous modifications had been made in the years that followed, including a 1978 addition that had been constructed by a builder.

For reasons of secrecy, however, Fritzl had built the

> **No matter how much Fritzl's neighbours gossiped about him, none of them had the faintest conception of what was taking place in his household**

bunker himself. It could only be reached by going down the cellar stairs, passing through a number of rooms and unlocking a series of eight doors. The final door was hidden behind a large shelving unit.

The bunker itself consisted of a kitchen, a bathroom, a living area and two bedrooms. There was no source of natural light, and the air was stale and stagnant. The ceiling was very low – it was less than 2 m (6 ft) high at best. It had not been difficult for Fritzl to construct the bunker. As an electrical engineer, he had always been good with his hands.

Good provider

Born in Amstetten on 9 April 1935, Fritzl had been raised alone by his mother after his father had deserted his small family. Josef Fritzl Snr went on to fight as a Nazi stormtrooper and was killed during the Second World War. The younger Josef had been a good student with a notable aptitude for technical matters. He had just begun his career with a Linz steel company when he married 17-year-old Rosemarie at the age of 21. The couple had two sons and five daughters together, including the beautiful Elisabeth.

Fritzl was a very good provider, but he was also an unpleasant husband and father. In 1967 he was sentenced to 18 months in prison after having confessed to the rape of a 24-year-old woman. After his release he was employed by a construction firm and later on he travelled throughout Austria as a technical equipment salesman. Until April 2008, the electrical engineer had no further brushes with the law. That is not to say that he led an exemplary life. Among his neighbours he had a reputation as an unfriendly man, one who kept himself to himself and his family away from others. There was talk that he was very firm with his children and that absolute obedience was expected.

No matter how much Fritzl's neighbours gossiped about him, none of them had the faintest conception of what was taking place in his household.

In 1977, Fritzl began sexually abusing Elisabeth. She was 11 years old at the time. Although she told no one, not even her close friend Christa Woldrich, it is easy to imagine what a devastating effect it must have had on her.

'I did get the impression that she felt more comfortable at school than at home,' Woldrich told one reporter. 'Sometimes she went quiet when it was time to go home again.'

In January 1983, Elisabeth ran away from home, ending up in Vienna. She was then 16 years old. Even though she tried her best to hide, she only managed to remain free for three weeks before the police found her and returned her to her parents.

The authorities calculate that Fritzl was well into the construction of the bunker at this point. Eighteen months after the police had brought the girl back to number 40 Ybbsstrasse, Elisabeth's incarceration began.

Fritzl appeared to be very open about what had happened to his 18-year-old daughter.

He told everyone that she had been a drug-taking problem child who had gone off to join a religious cult. But there was no cult, of course. Fritzl backed up his story by forcing Elisabeth to write a letter in which she told everyone not to search for her because she was now happy.

Elisabeth was alone in the bunker until the birth of her first child. Her only visitor was her father, who would arrive every few days to bring her food. He would then rape her. The nightmare became greater still during Elisabeth's fourth year underground when she became pregnant for the first time, suffering a miscarriage. Elisabeth's second pregnancy led to the birth of Kerstin and Stefan arrived in the following year. There would be seven children in all, including Michael, who died when he was three days old. While Kerstin, Stefan and Felix, the youngest, lived in captivity, Fritzl arranged for the others to be taken care of by Rosemarie.

It had been difficult to explain the babies away. After all, Rosemarie knew nothing of the bunker. Like everyone else, she believed the troubled Elisabeth had achieved some sort of happiness as a member of a fictitious cult. However, Fritzl had already laid the groundwork by portraying Elisabeth as an unstable and irresponsible daughter. All that remained was to smuggle the babies upstairs in the middle of the night and then leave them on the

Elisabeth Fritzl who now lives under an assumed name in an Austrian village known as 'Village X'

40 Ybbsstrasse, outwardly a normal house

A police van parked outside the back of the Fritzls' dwelling

front doorstep with a note from Elisabeth.

In May 1993, 9-month-old Lisa became the first of the grandchildren who would be cared for by Rosemarie. When Monika appeared in the following year, the press took note. 'What kind of mother would do such a thing?' asked one newspaper. After having raised seven of her own children, the neighbours took pity on Rosemarie. However, the senior citizen made no complaints and she proved to be devoted to her grandchildren. All three did well at school and they seemed happy and healthy, despite their incestuous background. Even the unfriendly Fritzl received a certain amount of respect and admiration for helping to raise three young children during the years in which one might rightly expect to take things easy.

For the children in the bunker, life could not have been more different. Kerstin, Stefan and Felix knew they had siblings living in the house above their heads. Indeed, Kerstin and Stefan could remember the babies being taken away.

To add insult to injury, Josef would bring videos that showed Lisa, Monika and Alexander enjoying a lifestyle that was vastly superior to their own.

Despite her suffering, Elisabeth did her best to provide Kerstin, Stefan and Felix with some semblance of a normal upbringing. She gave them regular lessons, in which they learned reading, writing and mathematics. All of the children, whether they were raised in the bunker by Elisabeth or upstairs by Rosemarie, ended up being intelligent, articulate and polite.

Bunker mentality

Fritzl has never explained why he took Lisa, Monika and Alexander upstairs, while keeping their siblings captive below. One possible explanation might have been lack of space. With a total area of around 35 m² (380 ft²) the bunker was becoming increasingly cramped, particularly when the children grew bigger.

After the birth of Monika in 1993, Fritzl alleviated the problem somewhat by expanding the size of the bunker to 55 m² (600 ft²).

On 27 April 2008, nine days after Fritzl had telephoned for an ambulance, a number of police officers arrived at the house of Josef and Rosemarie Fritzl. Josef Fritzl was taken into custody while Rosemarie and her grandchildren were taken to a psychiatric hospital, where they were reunited with Elisabeth.

On the day after his arrest, Fritzl confessed to keeping Elisabeth captive and fathering her children. He defended his actions by claiming that the sex had been consensual and that Elisabeth's incarceration had been necessary in order to rescue her from 'persons of questionable moral standards'. Elisabeth had refused to obey his rules ever since she had entered puberty, he said.

As Fritzl awaited trial for his crimes he became more and more enraged by the media coverage. Eventually, the electrical engineer released a letter through his lawyer in which he spoke of the kindness he had always shown his family. Fritzl pointed out that he could have killed them, but chose not to.

On 16 March 2009, the first day of his trial, Fritzl was charged with rape, incest, kidnapping, false imprisonment, slavery, grievous assault and the murder of baby Michael. He pleaded guilty to all of the charges with the exception of grievous assault and murder.

In keeping with the agreement she struck with the police on the day she finally emerged from the bunker, Elisabeth did not appear in court. Instead, the 42-year-old woman's testimony was presented in the form of an 11-hour video recording. The prosecution later revealed that Elisabeth had been watching the proceedings from the visitors' gallery. She had been heavily disguised to avoid being recognized.

The news caused Fritzl to break down. He changed his plea to guilty on all charges, thereby ending the court case. That same day he was sentenced to life imprisonment, with no possibility of parole for 15 years.

A forensic officer emerges from the Fritzls' front door

Danger signs: Indecently exposed himself as a young man

Pattern of crime: With the construction of the bunker, his need to control others was written in concrete

Breakthrough: When 19-year-old daughter Kerstin had to be taken to hospital, Fritzl's world began to unravel

Plea for the defence: 'I was born to rape. I could have behaved a lot worse than locking up my daughter'

Sentence: Life imprisonment (without the possibility of parole for 15 years)

THE MAN WITH NO FRIENDS

Thomas Hamilton

Name: Thomas Hamilton

DOB: 10 May 1952

Profession: Former shopkeeper

Upbringing: Born shortly before his parents separated; adopted by his grandparents at the age of 2; told that his mother was his sister

Category: Paedophile obsessed with guns and boys clubs

Number of victims: 17 killed, 15 injured

Though 43, Thomas Hamilton had never had any adult friends. He preferred to spend his time with young boys. He displayed all the signs of paedophilia, yet no reliable evidence has ever been produced that he sexually abused anyone.

Hamilton was born Thomas Watt on 10 May 1952 in Glasgow. Shortly thereafter, his parents separated and in 1955 were divorced. Just before his fourth birthday, he was adopted by his maternal grandparents, who changed his name to Thomas Watt Hamilton. He grew up believing that his birth mother was his sister. It wasn't until 1985, when Hamilton was in his 30s, that the woman he thought was his sister finally moved out of the parental home.

Two years later, Hamilton and his adoptive parents moved into the house in which he would live for the rest of his life. By the end of 1992, Hamilton's adoptive mother had died, while his adoptive father had moved into an old people's home. At the age of 40, he was for the first time living apart from his adoptive parents.

Hamilton had participated in boy scouts as a child, an interest that continued into adulthood. In 1973, he was appointed assistant scout leader of a troop in Stirling. Although he had passed the various checks made into his suitability, it wasn't long before complaints were being made about his leadership. The most serious of these concerned two occasions when boys were forced to sleep in a van overnight in his company. Confronted with the first complaint, Hamilton explained that the intended accommodation had been double-booked. When the situation repeated itself, an investigation was undertaken which revealed that there had been no booking on either occasion. As a result, he was removed from his position and, ultimately, his name was added to a blacklist.

In the years that followed, he made several attempts to return to scouting. In February 1977, Hamilton requested that a committee of inquiry be formed to address a complaint that he had been victimized. The request was denied. The following year, he failed in an attempt to bypass the blacklist by offering his services in another district.

Man among boys

Frustrated in his attempts to again participate in scouting, Hamilton became increasingly involved in boys' clubs. Beginning in the late 1970s, Hamilton organized and operated at least 15 different clubs, three of which, the Dunblane Boys' Club, the Falkirk Boys' Club and the Bishopbriggs Boys' Club, he was active in at the time of his death.

Hamilton's clubs were aimed primarily at boys between the ages of 8 and 11. For the most part, activities consisted of gymnastics and games. Although he was on occasion assisted by others, including parents, more often than not Hamilton ran each club entirely on his own. He employed a title, 'The Boys' Clubs Sports Group Committee', in order to create the impression that other adults were involved in the running of the clubs. In reality, there was no such body.

When he became unemployed in 1985, the fees provided Hamilton with a small source of income. In most cases, the clubs began as extremely popular operations – some attracting approximately 70 boys – but would invariably start to decline.

His ideas of discipline tended not to match those of the boys' parents. The fitness regimes were strenuous and harsh, leading volunteers and parents to consider them militaristic. Some went so far as to suggest that Hamilton was taking pleasure in dominating the boys.

> *Also disconcerting was his habit of taking photographs of the boys as they posed in their trunks. In 1989, he added video to his collection of images*

It was noted that Hamilton showed an unusual interest in certain boys, appearing to have favourites. He received complaints from some parents regarding his insistence that the boys wore tight black swimming trunks during gymnastics. Once these were provided by Hamilton, the boys were obliged to change in the gymnasium, rather than the changing rooms.

Also disconcerting was his habit of taking photographs of the boys as they posed in their trunks. In 1989, he added video to his collection of images. When confronted by parents, Hamilton would explain that the photographs and videos were taken for training and advertising purposes.

Those parents who saw the videos couldn't help but notice that the boys looked unhappy and uncomfortable. What's more, Hamilton's camerawork appeared to linger on certain parts of the boys' bodies. Hamilton's home contained

Hamilton was clearly a danger to youngsters, but nothing was done

support from parents. The lease was subsequently reinstated.

In addition to the boys' clubs, Hamilton would run summer camps. These usually catered for boys of about 9 years of age who might be 12 or so in number.

Exactly how many camps Hamilton ran is unknown. His claim that the July 1988 summer camp on Inchmoan Island on Loch Lomond was his 55th cannot be confirmed.

Nevertheless, it was the first to be visited by the authorities. Acting on a complaint, two police officers inspected the camp on 20 July, to find the boys ill-nourished and inadequately dressed. As one of the constables was involved in scouting, Hamilton dismissed their findings as part of a conspiracy launched by the Scouts' Association. After another of his summer camps, held in July 1991, was investigated, Hamilton replaced the programme with what he termed a 'residential sports training course', in which boys slept on the dining room floor of Dunblane High School. This, too, was investigated by the authorities.

Crossing the line

By 1995, the rumour and innuendo that Hamilton had complained about in letters to parents was putting an end to his clubs. Three had had to shut down due to declining enrolment, while a proposed

hundreds of photographs of boys – many wearing black swimming trunks – hanging on the walls or in albums.

Whenever a boy was pulled out of one of his clubs, Hamilton would respond by writing the parents long letters in which he would complain of the rumour and innuendo associated with his activities. He would often hand-deliver these intimidating letters at night.

There were some parents, however, who supported Hamilton. When, in 1983, his leases at two high schools were cancelled when former issues with the scouts came to light, Hamilton obtained 30 letters of

> *Two police officers inspected the camp that Hamilton ran on 20 July, to find the boys ill-nourished and inadequately dressed*

A photograph of the first-year class taken by teacher Gwen Mayor shortly before Hamilton killed her and 16 pupils at Dunblane Primary School

new club was cancelled when only one boy attended. On 18 August, he circulated letters in Dunblane intended to counter what he described as false and misleading gossip which had been circulated by scout officials. He sought to break free from his reputation by opening up a new boys' club some 40 km (25 miles) away in Bishopbriggs.

Complaints against Hamilton were now being made on a frequent basis. However, while his conduct was of great concern, it had not yet crossed the line into criminality.

At shortly after 8:00 on the morning of 13 March 1996, a neighbour saw Hamilton scraping ice off a white rental van outside his Stirling home. They shared what the neighbour would describe as a normal conversation.

Some time later Hamilton drove the van 10 km (6 miles) north to the town of Dunblane, arriving at about 9:30 in the car park of Dunblane Primary School, the site of his intended massacre.

Parking beside a telegraph pole, he cut the wires. It is supposed that Hamilton thought they served the school, when in fact they were for adjoining houses. Beneath his jacket he wore four holsters which held two 9 mm Browning semi-automatic pistols and two .357 Smith and Wesson revolvers. He was also wearing a woollen hat and ear protectors. Picking up a large camera bag, Hamilton walked across the

After Dunblane, Home Secretary Michael Howard implemented changes to the handgun laws

car park and entered the school by a side door.

It was a little more than half an hour into the school day when Hamilton entered the gymnasium. There he found two teachers, an assistant and a class of 28 pupils, ranging between 5 and 6 years of age. Hamilton walked forward a few steps, raised his pistol and began firing rapidly and indiscriminately. He hit the physical education teacher, Eileen Harrild, four times, including a shot to the left breast. The other teacher, 47-year-old Gwen Mayor, was killed instantly. The assistant, Mary Blake, was also shot, but managed to seek refuge with several children in a storage area, out of the line of direct fire.

Hamilton remained in his position and continued to shoot, killing one child and injuring others. Still firing indiscriminately, he began to advance further into the gymnasium. He then walked over to a group of the injured and fired at point-blank range.

Although he resumed the wholesale firing, some of Hamilton's shots were more directed. He fired at one boy who was passing by the gymnasium, but missed. Another shot was taken through a window, and was probably directed at an adult who was walking across the playground. Again, he missed.

He walked out of the gymnasium and fired four shots towards the school library, hitting a staff member, Grace Tweddle, in the head.

He then sprayed the outside of a classroom hut, but hit no one. The teacher, Catherine Gordon, had instructed her pupils to get down on the floor just moments before the shots entered the classroom.

Hamilton re-entered the gymnasium, again shooting haphazardly. He then dropped the pistol and drew a revolver. Placing the muzzle in his mouth, he pulled the trigger.

It is estimated that Hamilton's rampage lasted between three and four minutes and the damage that he caused during that time was absolutely appalling.

On the floor of the gymnasium 15 children and their teacher, Gwen Mayor, lay dead. Hamilton had shot these 16 people a total of 58 times. One more child, Mhairi Isabel MacBeath, would die on the way to hospital; 13 other people had received wounds.

All were taken to Stirling Royal Infirmary.

As great as the carnage was, it could have been much, much worse. It wasn't until 9:41, approximately one minute after Hamilton had killed himself, that police received an emergency call.

The first officers arrived on the scene at 9:50. Hamilton was shown to have entered the school with 743 rounds of ammunition, of which he used 106. He used only one of the two 9 mm Browning semi-automatic pistols.

Both .357 Smith and Wesson revolvers remained in their holsters until Hamilton used one to commit suicide.

Danger signs: Dismissed as a scout leader because of concerns about his 'moral intentions towards boys'; investigations into his activities by Central Scotland Police

Planning the crime: Less than six months before the murders, Hamilton increased the size of his weapons collection; he quizzed a pupil every week for two years about the layout of the gym and the school routine

Aftermath: The UK's handgun laws were tightened up; a handgun amnesty resulted in 160,000 weapons being handed in to police

THE SCHIZOID 'BISHOP'

Gary Heidnik

Name: Gary Heidnik

DOB: 22 November 1943

Profession: Psychiatric nurse, investor

Upbringing: Placed in care when young because of mother's alcoholism

Category: Diagnosed with schizoid personality disorder and discharged from military service; IQ of 130

Previous charges: Arrested for kidnapping and raping his lover's mentally retarded sister

Number of victims: 2 killed, 6 kidnapped

Ellen Heidnik drank during her pregnancies. She drank a lot. Even at a time when the sight of a pregnant woman holding a wine glass was not unusual, Ellen stood out from the crowd. By the time her first child, Gary, was born – on 22 November 1943 in Eastlake, Ohio – Ellen's alcoholism had already begun to affect her marriage. Two years and one more son later, her husband filed for divorce.

The effects of the split overshadowed Gary's early years, as well as his brother Terry's.

Initially, the two boys stayed with their unstable, unreliable mother, but when she remarried they were sent to live with their father, Michael Heidnik, and his new wife.

Misshapen head

They were very unhappy times for Gary. He disliked his stepmother and he was brutalized by his disciplinarian of a father. He was often punished for wetting his bed and suffered even further when his father deliberately hung the stained sheets out of the second-floor bedroom window for all the neighbours to see. Horrendous as this experience was for Gary, it was nothing compared to the terror he felt when Michael dangled him by his ankles in place of the sheets.

School was no better. Gary was not only taunted for the bed-wetting – he was also mocked because of his unusual appearance. As a young child he had fallen out of a tree, which had left him with a slightly misshapen head. Michael made his son's schooldays all the worse by painting bull's-eyes on the seat of his trousers, thereby creating a target for the bullies. In spite of all of these drawbacks, Gary excelled in the classroom. He was invariably at the top of his class and his IQ was once measured at 130.

His intelligence, combined with his status as an outcast, might have contributed to his unusual ambitions. While so many of his male classmates dreamed of becoming baseball players and stars of football, 12-year-old Gary's twin aspirations were the achievement of great wealth and a career in the military. He made an early start by entering Virginia's Staunton Military Academy at the age of 14. Once again Gary proved to be an excellent student. However, unlike Barry Goldwater and John Dean, two of the school's illustrious alumni, Gary never graduated from the prestigious school. After two years of study he left the academy, returning to his father's house. He attempted to resume his studies at a couple of different high schools, but he felt that he was learning nothing, so at the age of 18 he dropped out of school and joined the army.

Though he made few friends amongst his comrades, Gary shone in the military. After completing basic training, he was sent to San Antonio in Texas, where he was to become a medical orderly. Now that his military career seemed well and truly on its way, Gary began pursuing his other long-held dream – to become wealthy. He supplemented his pay by making loans with interest to his fellow soldiers. Though his modest business would have been frowned upon by his superiors, Gary was otherwise an exemplary and intelligent military man. In 1962, while at a field hospital in West Germany, he achieved a near-perfect score in his high school equivalency examination.

A few months later it was all over.

In August, Gary began to complain of nausea, dizziness and blurred vision. The doctors who attended him identified two causes – stomach flu and 'schizoid personality disorder'. Before the year was up, he had been shipped back home. He was granted an honourable discharge and a disability pension. With one of his two dreams dashed into smithereens, Gary enrolled at the University of Pennsylvania. His chosen courses – chemistry, history, anthropology and biology – were so diverse in nature that it appeared that he was looking for direction. If so, Gary was unsuccessful. Using his army medical training, he worked for a time at two Philadelphia

> *Now without work, Heidnik's eccentricities grew, while his personal hygiene declined. If he did not want to be disturbed, he would roll up one trouser leg as a signal to others*

hospitals, but he proved to be a poor worker.

Now without work and living on his pension his eccentricities grew, while his personal hygiene declined. Gary found a leather jacket, which he would wear regardless of the weather or the social situation. If he did not want to be disturbed, he would roll up one trouser leg as a signal to others. Then there were the suicide attempts – not just

Heidnik used an unlicensed gun to shoot one of his tenants in the face

Gary's, but those of his brother and his mother, too. These were so frequent that they could be numbered in the dozens, but only Ellen was successful. In 1970, the four-times married alcoholic took her own life by drinking mercury.

Both Heidnik boys spent years moving in and out of mental institutions. Yet despite his many periods of confinement, Gary managed to begin amassing the wealth he had sought since he was a child. In 1971 he founded his own church, the United Church of the Ministers of God, and he ordained himself as its bishop. Although Gary had just four followers, they included two people who were close to him – his mentally retarded girlfriend and his brother.

Out of control

As a self-anointed minister, Gary began investing in earnest. He bought property and played the stock market, making a great deal of money when Hugh Hefner's Playboy empire went public in 1971. But all of the time he was spinning increasingly out of control. Gary became one of those individuals who is often described as 'known to the police'. There were any number of reasons for his notoriety. In 1976, for example, he used an unlicensed gun to shoot one of his tenants in the face. Incredibly, it was not until 1978 that he first went to jail. But the three- to seven-year sentence had nothing to do with the earlier shooting. Instead, Gary had been found guilty of kidnapping, unlawful restraint, false imprisonment, rape, involuntary deviate sexual intercourse and interfering with the custody of a committed person.

All of this had come about because Gary had signed his girlfriend's sister out of a mental institution and had kept her confined to his basement. Not only had he raped the young woman but he had infected her with gonorrhoea. In the middle of what turned out to be four years of incarceration, he handed a prison guard a note explaining that he could no longer speak because Satan had shoved a cookie down his throat. Gary remained silent for over 27 months.

When he was finally released in April 1983, he returned to Philadelphia and resumed his role as a bishop with the United Church of the Ministers of God. Even though Gary's congregation had not grown much, from time to time it included mentally retarded women, whom he would impregnate.

It is hardly surprising that Betty Disto, Gary's first bride, was not immediately aware of his odd behaviour and poor hygiene because the couple had become engaged before they had even laid eyes on one another. The couple had met through a matrimonial service. They had been corresponding for two years when, in September of 1985, Betty flew from her address in the Philippines to the United States. Their October marriage lasted for just three months. Betty could not stand to see her groom in bed with other women, but she had no choice because Gary made her watch. Beaten, raped and threatened, a pregnant Betty fled home with the help of the local Filipino community.

Betty made her escape in the first few days of 1986, but Gary's life really began to fall apart towards the end of that year. On the evening of 26 November 1986, Gary abducted his first victim, a prostitute named Josefina Rivera. It all happened gradually.

She had been standing outside in the cold rain when Gary picked her up in his Cadillac Coupe De Ville. On the way, he stopped at McDonald's and bought her a coffee. She did not object when he took her to his home, a run-down house at 3520 North Marshall Street.

The neighbourhood had seen better days – drug dealers worked its streets

There was something surreal about it all. Gary's house had seen better days, as had the rest of the neighbourhood. Decades earlier, the area had housed working-class German immigrants. The streets had been spotless then, but now they were pockmarked and covered in litter. Drug dealers worked its streets selling crack cocaine and marijuana to passing motorists and poverty was everywhere, yet Gary had a Rolls-Royce in his garage.

The door to his home was like something from a children's movie. When it opened, Josefina noticed that Gary had glued thousands of pennies to the walls of his kitchen. As he led her upstairs to the bedroom, she realized that the hallway had been wallpapered with $5 bills. In many ways, the house was a reflection of its owner. Gary's gold jewellery and Rolex watch contrasted sharply with his worn and stained clothing.

Like the rest of the house, the bedroom was sparsely furnished. There was nothing more than a waterbed, two chairs and a dresser. Gary gave Josefina the money they had agreed upon – $20 – and then he got undressed. The energetic and emotionless sex act was over in a matter of minutes. Josefina had felt a little uneasy about Gary, but what happened next took her by surprise. He grabbed her by the throat and choked her until she blacked out. Brief as it was, her loss of consciousness provided Gary with enough time to handcuff her.

Josefina was ordered to her feet and then she was marched downstairs to the basement. The unfinished room was cold, clammy and filthy, much like the old mattress that he made her sit on, and the floor was concrete, though some of the surface had been removed. After attaching metal clamps and chains to Josefina's ankles, Gary got down to digging the exposed earth.

He talked as he worked, telling the shackled woman that he had fathered four children by four different women, but it had all gone wrong. He had no contact with any of his offspring and yet he really wanted and *deserved* a family.

'Society owes me a wife and a big family,' was how he put it. 'I want to get ten women and keep them here and get them all pregnant. Then, when they have babies, I want to raise those children here too. We'll be like one big happy family.'

And with that bit of information, he raped her.

After attaching clamps and chains to Josefina's ankles, Heidnik began digging

Screaming blue murder

Once she was alone, Josefina tried to escape. After freeing one of her ankles, she managed to prise open one of the basement windows and squeeze through it. Then she was out in the open. She crawled as far as the chain around her other ankle allowed her to and then she screamed at the top of her voice. But in Gary's neighbourhood screams like Josefina's were an everyday thing. The only person

> **By 7 February, Sandra had completely lost consciousness. At this point, Gary finally removed the handcuff that had kept her dangling and she fell into a heap on the concrete floor**

who paid any attention to the sound was Gary.

He ran downstairs, grabbed the chain and pulled her back into the basement. The filthy mattress was too good for her now. Dragging her across the cement floor, he threw her into the shallow pit. She was covered over with a sheet of plywood, upon which Gary placed heavy weights.

On her third day of captivity she was joined by a mentally retarded young woman named Sandra Lindsay. The girl seemed to have a very limited understanding of what was happening, so it was easy for Gary to get her to write a short note home. *'Dear Mom, do not worry. I will call.'*

It was the last time Sandra's mother would ever hear from her daughter. Josefina and Sandra spent weeks together. Sometimes they were in the pit and sometimes they were chained to pipes in the basement. They endured repeated rapes, beatings and the ever-present cold.

On 22 December they were joined by 19-year-old Lisa Thomas, a third 'wife'. Gary lured the girl to 3520 North Marshall Street with offers of food and clothing and a trip to Atlantic City. In the end she only got the food and a spiked glass of wine. After she passed out, Gary raped her and then took her down to the basement.

On New Year's Day Gary abducted a fourth woman, but 23-year-old Deborah Dudley was totally unlike his other 'wives'. Ignoring the consequences, she fought back at nearly every opportunity. Her disobedience invariably led to the other three captives being beaten as well, which created disorder and tension within the group.

When Gary began to encourage the women to report on each other, Josefina saw an opportunity to gain Gary's trust. Though she continued to suffer at his hands, Gary came to believe that Josefina actually took pleasure in her circumstance.

Wife number five, 18-year-old Jacqueline Askins, arrived on 18 January. After raping and shackling the girl, Gary surprised his 'wives' with generous helpings of Chinese food and a bottle of champagne. After weeks of bread, water and stale hot dogs, it seemed like the most elaborate feast.

To what did they owe this unexpected treat? It was Josefina's birthday.

Wicked punishment

However, any hopes that Gary might be softening were soon dashed. If anything, his abuse escalated. When he caught Sandra Lindsay trying to remove the plywood covering from the pit, she was forced to hang by one of her wrists from a ceiling beam.

She responded by going on a hunger strike, but

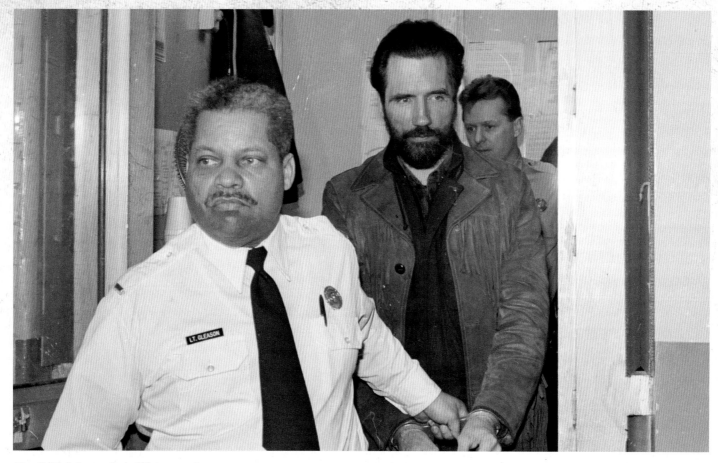

Gary Heidnik is marched off into custody

after a few days she appeared incapable of eating. When Gary tried to force food down her throat, she vomited.

By 7 February, Sandra had completely lost consciousness. At this point, Gary finally removed the handcuff that had kept her dangling and she fell into a heap on the concrete floor.

Kicking her into the pit, he assured his other wives that Sandra was faking. It was probably a matter of minutes later that Sandra died.

The women watched as Gary carried Sandra's body upstairs and then they heard the sound of a power saw. Later that day, one of his dogs entered the basement, tail wagging. In its mouth was a bone covered in fresh meat.

Within days, the house and the basement took on a foul odour. Gary was finding it hard to dispose of Sandra's remains. Using his food processor he ground up what he could, feeding the meat to his dogs and his wives – but some body parts were very difficult to deal with.

Sandra's severed head sat in a pot of boiling water for days, while her ribcage was broiled in the oven. The smell spread to some of the adjoining properties, which led to complaints from the neighbours. Although the police investigated they believed Gary's story that he had cooked some bad meat. Meanwhile, the torture endured by the women became even more intense. Gary began poking their ears with a screwdriver, in the belief that deaf wives would be easier to control. He also stripped the insulation from extension cords in order to shock his captives.

Josefina was not only spared these punishments, she became an administrator. On 18 March she helped with an elaborate method of torture. First of all the pit was flooded and then the other wives, still in chains, were forced into the water. After that the plywood covering was put in place and weighed down. Finally, the bare wire of the extension cord was pushed through a hole, thereby electrocuting the women.

The second of these shocks killed Deborah Dudley. Her death marked a significant change in Gary's relationship with Josefina.

In his eyes, her participation in the torture, combined with Deborah's death, meant she could be blackmailed. That made her trustworthy – or so he thought. For the first time in almost four months she was allowed to leave the basement. She shared Gary's bed, dined with him at restaurants and helped with his grocery shopping. Josefina even went so far as to accompany Gary to the country, where he disposed of Deborah's body.

On 24 March 1987, the day after she helped abduct a new woman, Agnes Adams, Josefina convinced Gary to let her visit her children. She promised him that she would return with yet another 'wife'. Gary dropped her off and waited in the car for her return. But Josefina did not visit her children – she had none. Instead, she sprinted to her boyfriend's apartment, where she poured out her bizarre and almost unbelievable story.

After the police arrived and noted the scarring that had been left by months of wearing heavy chains, they arrested Gary. His surviving 'wives' were rescued when the police converged on 3520 North Marshall Street on the following morning.

Gary's trial began on 20 June 1988. From the start, his defence lawyers attempted to prove that the one-time medical assistant was insane. They called a psychiatrist and a psychologist to the stand, but their efforts were in vain. Ten days later he was found guilty of two counts of first-degree murder, four counts of aggravated assault, five counts of rape, six counts of kidnapping and one count of involuntary deviate sexual intercourse. He was subsequently sentenced to death.

On the evening of 6 July 1999, 11 years after he had been sentenced, Gary Heidnik was executed by lethal injection. It is hardly surprising that his body was not claimed by the other members of his family.

Michael Heidnik, his father, had not seen him since the early 1960s. When he heard about the death sentence he made a brief statement to the press.

'I'm not interested. I don't care. It don't bother me a bit.'

Danger signs: Charged with aggravated assault after shooting at one of his tenants in 1976; wallpapered his hallway with US banknotes; had a serious obsession with locks and keys; invented and ran his own church

Pattern of crime: Moving on from spousal rape and assault, became serial rapist and imprisoner

Breakthrough: Heidnik allowed his 'girlfriend' to visit her family; she went straight to the police

Sentence: The death penalty (his last meal was two cups of black coffee and four pieces of pizza)

DAVID PARKER RAY

David Parker Ray

Name:	David Parker Ray
DOB:	6 November 1939
Profession:	Motor mechanic
Category:	Organized lust killer with several partners
Upbringing:	Raised by grandfather; teased for being shy with girls
Previous record:	Brushes with the law over drug and alcohol abuse
Number of victims:	14 to 60

Truth or Consequences, New Mexico was once a place of relaxation. The first people to enjoy its hospitality arrived over one hundred years ago. They were there to soak in the Geronimo Springs at John Cross Ranch. It would be the first of several dozen spas to be built around the heated groundwater that continues to bubble up in this city of less than 8,000 souls. The entire community was built around this natural phenomenon. Anyone who wonders how important it once was to the local economy need look no further than the city's original name: Hot Springs. The city became Truth or Consequences in 1950, when the popular radio quiz show of that name offered to broadcast from the first community to rename itself after the show. It was all good fun.

The first indication of David Parker Ray's crimes came on 26 July 1996, when the sheriff's office in Truth or Consequences received a call from a young Marine. On the previous day he had argued with his wife Kelly Van Cleave and he had not seen or heard from her since. The anxious husband received only advice.

His wife had been gone such a short time that she could not be considered as a missing person. Based on past experience, the office had every reason to believe that Kelly would turn up.

Sure enough, the young man's wife returned home on the very next day. She had been brought back by an employee of nearby Elephant Butte State Park, where she had been found wandering in a dazed and incoherent state.

Kelly could account for only a few of the many hours she had been missing. After the fight with her husband, she remembered going to a friend's house. This was followed by trips to a number of bars, the last of which was the Blue Waters Saloon. It was there that Kelly ordered a beer, her first drink of the evening.

She soon began to feel dizzy. The sensation was not dissimilar to being drunk, but something was not quite right. Kelly could recall little else from this point onwards, though she was certain that an old friend, Jesse Ray, had offered to help. Those missing hours brought an end to Kelly's marriage. Her husband could never accept her disappearance, or her claim that she could not remember what had happened.

Nightmares

Jesse Ray might have been able to help... but she could not be found. Kelly soon left Truth or Consequences, never to return. She would never see Jesse again.

Now separated, Kelly began to suffer from nightmares. The horrifying images were remarkably consistent – she saw herself being tied to a table, being gagged with duct tape and having a knife held to her throat. Nothing quite made sense so Kelly never did report her strange experience to the authorities. All the sheriff's office at Truth or Consequences had on file was a seemingly trivial phone call from a distrusting husband. They could not have known that the woman who walked through their door on 7 July 1997 was bringing information that was related to Kelly's disappearance.

The woman had come to report that she had not heard from her 22-year-old daughter, Marie Parker, for several days. This time, there would be an investigation. In such a small city, it was not difficult to track the young woman's movements. Marie had last been seen on 5 July at the Blue Waters Saloon. She had been drinking with Jesse Ray. Jesse told the

Elephant Butte State Park: Kelly Cleave went missing and was found wandering in a dazed and incoherent state near here

authorities that Marie had been drinking heavily so she had driven her home, but she had not seen her since.

But Jesse was not the only person that Marie had been drinking with on the night of her disappearance. Roy Yancy, an old boyfriend, had also been raising a glass at the Blue Waters Saloon. A Truth or Consequences boy born and raised, there was nothing in Roy's past to make the community proud.

As a child he had been part of a gang that had roamed Truth or Consequences strangling cats, poisoning dogs and tipping over gravestones, acts that led the city to cancel that year's Hallowe'en festivities. He had also received a dishonourable discharge from the navy.

Marie might well have been in the company of an unsavoury character, but the Truth or Consequences sheriff's office saw nothing unusual about her disappearance. After all, the city was known for its transient population. They were all too ready to accept someone's hazy recollection of a girl accepting a ride out of the city. It was a typical story.

At around this time a new woman arrived in the small city. Cindy Hendy's history was anything but enviable. A victim of sexual abuse, she had been molested by her stepfather before being turned out on the street at the age of 11. Cindy had been a teenage mother, but only in the sense that she had given birth – other people had taken on the job of raising her daughter. When she arrived in Truth or Consequences, Cindy was on the run from a drugs charge. Several months earlier, she had supplied cocaine to an undercover agent. She was a violent woman with a short fuse, so it was not long before she found herself in the local jail. Days later she was sent out to Elephant Butte Lake on a work-release

Police say David Parker Ray may have killed as many as 60 people in the small city of Truth or Consequences

programme. It was there that she first met David Parker Ray, the father of her friend Jesse.

He was a quiet, though approachable and friendly man. Ray had been a neglected child. Unloved by his mother, his only real contact with his drifter father came in the form of periodic drunken visits. These invariably ended with the old man leaving behind a bag of pornographic magazines that portrayed sadomasochistic acts. His adult life was one of many marriages and many jobs. He had lived a transient life before 1984, when he settled down with his fourth wife in Elephant Butte. After acquiring a run-down bungalow on a little piece of property, Ray supported them by working as an aircraft engine repairman.

By 1995, his wife had left him. The fourth Mrs Ray would be the final Mrs Ray, but she was not his last companion. In January 1999, Cindy Hendy moved into Ray's bungalow. It mattered little that he was two decades older because the 38-year-old had met her soulmate – someone who, like herself, was obsessed with sadomasochistic sex.

Lonely newcomer

Cindy had been living with Ray for just one month when, on 16 February, she invited Angie Montano over for a visit. Angie, a single mother, was new to Truth or Consequences, and was eager to make friends. She had come to the wrong place, because she was blindfolded, strapped to a bed and sexually assaulted. Ray and Cindy's sadistic tastes went beyond rape. Angie was stunned by cattle prods and various other devices that Ray had made himself. After five days, Angie managed to get Ray to agree to her release. He drove her to the nearest highway and let her out. As luck would have it, she was picked up by a passing off-duty police officer.

Angie shared her story with him, but she would not agree to making an official report. Just as Kelly Van Cleave had done four years earlier, Angie left Truth or Consequences, never to return.

Even as the assaults on Angie Montano were taking place, Cindy's mind was sometimes elsewhere. Though her 39th birthday had only just passed, she was about to become a grandmother. She made plans to attend the birth in her old home town of Monroe, Washington, but before she could go she needed to find a sex slave for Ray, someone who would meet his needs in her absence.

> *Cindy was about to become a grandmother and made plans to attend the birth, but before she could go she needed to find a sex slave for Ray*

On 18 March, they drove through the streets of Albuquerque in Ray's motorhome, where they came upon Cynthia Vigil. She was a prostitute, so it was not difficult to get her into the vehicle, nor was it hard to overpower the 22-year-old. After being bound, Cynthia was taken back to the Elephant Butte bungalow, where she was collared, chained, blindfolded and gagged. A tape was then played to her. The voice was Ray's.

'Hello, bitch. Well, this tape's gettin' played again. Must mean I picked up another hooker. And I'll bet you wonder what the hell's goin' on here.'

Those were just the first few sentences in a recording that lasted over five minutes. Ray went on to describe how he and his 'lady friend' were going to rape and torture the listener.

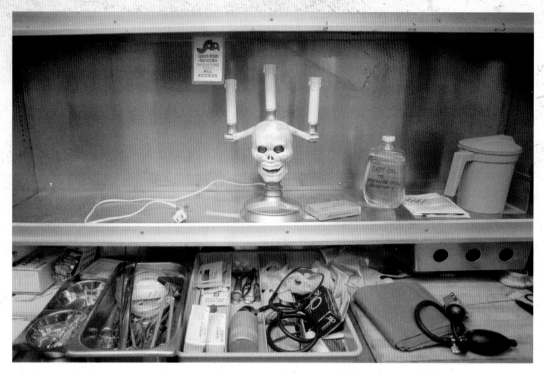

The 'Toy Box', a mobile torture trailer, was Ray's pride and joy – he invested $100,000 in it

quickly grabbed it and stabbed her abductor in the back of the neck.

It was not a lethal blow, but it was enough to give Cynthia time to get out of the house. Naked except for a dog collar and chain, she ran out of the door and down the dusty, unpaved street. She was spotted by the drivers of two cars, but they just swerved to avoid the distressed, bleeding woman.

After about a mile, she came upon a trailer home. She burst through the door and fell at the feet of a woman watching television.

'The gag is necessary,' he explained, 'because after a while you're goin' to be doin' a lot of screaming.'

True to the words of the tape, Ray and Cindy tortured and raped the prostitute over the course of the next three days. The assaults had no effect on Ray's work habits. As the fourth day began, he donned his state park uniform and drove off. Cindy was charged with keeping their victim under control. But his lady friend wasn't quite up to the task. In fact, she was downright sloppy.

When Cindy left the room to prepare a lunch of tuna sandwiches, the young prostitute noticed that her abductor had left behind the keys to her chains. After releasing herself, she grabbed the phone and called the Sierra County Sheriff's Office. Before she could say a word, Cindy was back in the room, bottle in hand. She took a violent swing at the prostitute, cutting her with the breaking glass. Cynthia noticed an ice pick while she was lying on the floor. She

Scene of the crime

Just minutes after the first interrupted call, the Sierra County Sheriff's Office received a second one. When the authorities arrived at the mobile home they heard a horrific tale of torture and assault. As Cynthia Vigil was being transported to the local hospital, the sheriff's department decided to call in the state police.

Over a dozen officers converged on Ray's bungalow, only to find that Cindy had fled.

The house was a mess, with garbage littering the floor. If there was any order, it was found in Ray's instruments of torture, which were arranged on hooks hanging from the walls of several rooms. His library included books on Satanism, torture and violent pornography. There were also a number of medical books, which presumably enabled him to carry out many of his fantasies.

The hunt was now on for Ray and Cindy. The chase was as short as it was easy. The couple had not fled – instead, they were driving along the nearby roads, looking for their captive. Ray and Cindy were spotted within 15 minutes, a mere two blocks from their home. They quickly admitted that they had been looking for Cynthia Vigil, but they also came up with an implausible explanation for their actions. The abduction of the prostitute had been a humanitarian act, claimed Ray and Cindy. Her confinement had been nothing more than an effort to help the young woman kick her addiction to heroin.

The story fooled no one. Ray and Cindy were arrested and taken into custody. As the investigation of Ray's property began, the state law enforcement officials realized that they did not have the resources to deal with their discoveries. Lieutenant Richard Libicer of the New Mexico State Police explained the situation:

I think it's safe to say that nothing that was inside that house was anything any of us had experienced before – or come across before – except maybe in a movie somewhere. It was just completely out of the realm of our experience.

The assortment of shackles and pulleys and other instruments of torture inside the bungalow appeared almost mundane compared to what was discovered inside a padlocked semi-trailer that was parked outside.

What Ray described as the 'Toy Box' contained hundreds of torture devices. Many of them, such as a machine that was used to electrocute women's breasts, had been designed and built by the former mechanic. At the centre of this horror was a gynaecology table. Cameras were installed, so that the women could see what was happening to them. Ray had also videotaped his assaults, including the one involving Kelly Van Cleave. She had supposedly been found wandering by a state park official – but the state park official was David Parker Ray.

The videotapes were a revelation. For a start, they linked Jesse Ray

The New Mexico State Police display the gynaecology table that Ray built

to her father's crimes. Kelly's evidence also proved useful, but the most damning testimony came from Cindy Hendy.

Within days of her arrest, the 39-year-old turned on her boyfriend. She told the investigators that Ray had been abducting and torturing women for many years. What is more, Ray had told Cindy that his fantasies had often ended in murder.

Subsequent searches of Elephant Butte Lake and the surrounding countryside revealed nothing, but the police remain convinced that Ray has killed at least one person. Cindy also confirmed that Jesse had participated in at least some of the abductions. She added that she often worked in tandem with Roy Yancy.

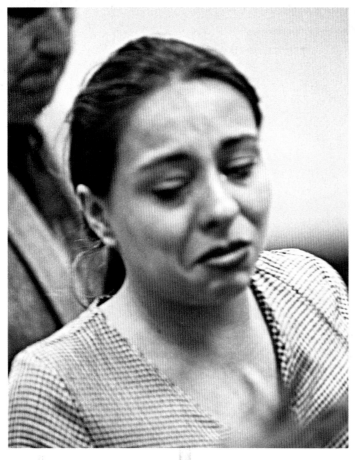

Victim Cynthia Vigil escaped naked with a metal collar round her neck

Soft centre

Despite his tough demeanour, Roy caved in when he was arrested. He told the police that he and Jesse had drugged Marie Parker, the young woman who had gone missing three years earlier. They had taken her to Elephant Butte, where she was tortured. When Ray tired of her, he instructed Roy to kill the woman who had once been his girlfriend.

The body was never found.

Roy Yancy pleaded guilty to second-degree murder and was sentenced to 20 years in prison.

After pleading guilty to kidnapping Kelly Van Cleave and Marie Parker, Jesse Ray received a nine-year sentence.

Facing the possibility of 197 years in prison, Cindy Hendy made a deal with the prosecutors. After pleading guilty to her crimes against Cynthia Vigil she received a 36-year sentence, with a further 18 years on probation.

Even Ray appeared to co-operate with the authorities, but only to the extent of describing his fantasies. He denied that he had abducted or murdered anyone. Any sadomasochistic activities had been between consenting adults. 'I got pleasure out of the woman getting pleasure,' he told one investigator. 'I did what they wanted me to do.'

Ray faced three trials for his crimes against Kelly Van Cleave, Cynthia Vigil and Angie Montano. He was found guilty in the first trial, but part of the way through the second he too made a deal. Ray agreed to plead guilty in exchange for Jesse's release. The case concerning Angie Montano was never heard because she had died of cancer.

On 30 September 2001, David Parker Ray received a 224-year sentence for his crimes against Kelly Van Cleave and Cynthia Vigil. In the end, Ray did not serve so much as a year. On 28 May 2002 he slumped

Jesse Ray, nicknamed 'Dyke on a Bike', abducted women for her father

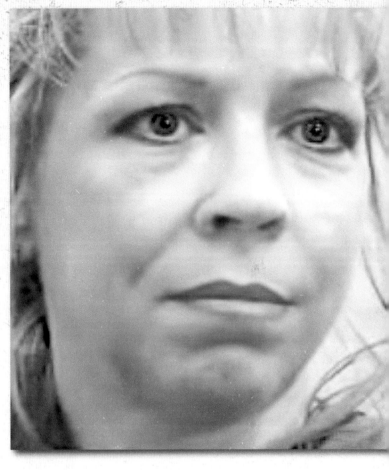

Cindy Hendy was molested by her stepfather and turned out on the street at the age of 11

over in a holding cell, killed by a massive heart attack.

'Satan has a place for you. I hope you burn in hell forever,' Cynthia Vigil's grandmother had once yelled at him.

One wonders whether the words meant anything to Ray. The one sign he had put up in his 'Toy Box' read: 'SATAN'S DEN'.

Danger signs: Collected sadistic implements which he called his 'friends'

Pattern of crime: Escalation of abduction and sexual torture of women

Breakthrough: The escape of victim, Cynthia Vigil, from captivity

Plea for the defence: 'My arrest has given me the time to reflect, read my Bible and get right with God'

Sentence: 224 years in prison (Ray died of a heart attack after eight months)

TEARS OF A TORTURER

Name: Cameron Hooker

DOB: 5 November 1953

Profession: Lumber mill worker

Upbringing: Shy, repressed childhood

Category: Violent sexual sadist hooked on pornography

Number of victims: 1

Cameron Hooker

Cameron Hooker seemed like a pretty regular guy. He was slightly gawky-looking and not particularly intelligent, but he was no dummy either. The most you could say about Cameron was that he was good with his hands. It was a skill that would enable him to pursue his fantasies and bring about a seven-year nightmare for one very unfortunate young woman.

Cameron was born in 1953 in the small Californian city of Alturas, though he spent much of his youth in the marginally larger community of Red Bluff. An unremarkable student, he began working at a local lumber mill while attending high school. He spent much of the money he earned on the sort of pornography that was produced for those with a leaning towards sadism and masochism. Cameron kept his fantasies secret until the age of 19, when he met Janice. Four years his junior, she was a plain, shy, insecure high school girl with little experience of the opposite sex. Cameron believed that he had found someone who could be moulded to fulfil his desires. After a period of polite dating, he introduced Janice to a series of violent sexual acts, which involved bondage, flogging and near-asphyxiation.

In 1975, two years into the relationship, Cameron married Janice. However, even at the wedding, he had begun to tire of his teenage bride. Her submissive nature did not quite fit his fantasies. What Cameron wanted was a sex slave. And Janice? What did she want? Janice wanted a baby.

Janice Hooker leaves court in Red Bluff, CA after giving testimony

The young couple struck a bargain. Janice could have her child if Cameron could have a sex slave. Throughout his wife's pregnancy, the lumber mill worker built a number of wooden boxes, each of them designed to confine a victim and muffle their cries for help. Cameron went about his preparations with great care, all the while making sure that no one could see what was going on at the rented Red Bluff house. Such was his dedication that the arrival of the couple's child – Janice's child, really – did little to alter his plans. Cameron would not be rushed – everything had to be just right.

It was not until several months after the birth that Cameron went out and got his slave. Janice went along for the ride. Indeed, it might be said that she was used as a lure. Who would suspect a woman with a baby in her arms?

The woman that Cameron would call his slave was Colleen Stan, an attractive 20-year-old from Eugene, Oregon. On the morning of Thursday 19 May 1977 she left her home to visit a friend in Westwood, California, some 500 miles (800 km) to the south.

It did not worry Colleen that she had no car and little money, because she considered herself an experienced hitchhiker. By the middle of the afternoon the young woman had travelled nearly 350 miles (560 km) to Red Bluff, just an hour and a half west of her final destination. Colleen's arrival in this small Californian community marked the beginning of the final and most challenging leg of her trip. Up until this point, she had been travelling along the busy Interstate 5 (I-5), where rides were plentiful, but now she had to use the less-travelled State Route 36, which would take her into Westwood.

With the end of the journey in sight, the seasoned Colleen continued to show great caution, turning down the first two offers of rides. The third car to stop was Cameron's blue Dodge Colt. When she realized that the smiling man at the wheel was accompanied by a mother and child, all of her fears melted away. But Colleen gradually began to feel uneasy. She noticed that Cameron constantly stared at her through the rear-view mirror.

Under normal circumstances this type of warning sign would have prompted her to look for a way out. In fact, when the car stopped at a service station Colleen sought refuge in the toilets and considered escaping.

'A voice told me to run and jump out a window and never look back,' she later recalled.

But then there was the wife and the baby – surely the leering young man would not do anything with them around.

So Colleen returned to the car, unaware that she would not be free again for a long time. Just moments after pulling away from the service station, the Hookers talked about making a quick visit to some nearby ice caves. Cameron turned the Dodge on to a dirt road and after several minutes he brought it to a halt. The Hookers and their baby got out of the car, but Cameron returned. Jumping into the back seat, he pointed a knife at Colleen's throat. Terrified and fearing death, she allowed herself to be handcuffed, blindfolded and gagged. Cameron then locked a heavy, insulated plywood box around her head.

After Janice and the baby had returned to the car, Cameron turned it around and headed back to Red Bluff with his trophy – though he stopped for some fast food along the way.

Once home, Cameron led Colleen into his basement, where he strung her up by the wrists before stripping off her clothing and whipping her.

Where was Janice in all of this? Presumably she was upstairs with the baby – though she came down to the basement to have sex with her husband as Colleen hung suspended in front of them. After the couple had finished, Cameron released Colleen's wrists and forced her into a coffin-like box. Then he once again locked the small plywood box around her head before leaving.

The initial horror that Colleen had experienced marked the beginning of a routine that consisted of whippings, beatings, choking, burning and electrocution.

Colleen Stan was imprisoned by the Hookers for over seven years

When she was not being subjected to these tortures, Colleen was chained up in the larger of the two boxes. Eventually, Cameron constructed a small cell under the basement staircase, where he set his slave to work, shelling nuts and other menial tasks.

Weird contract

After seven months had passed, Colleen was presented with a contract stating that she agreed to become Cameron's slave. Although it was just a simple piece of paper, the document marked the point at which Colleen's nightmare intensified. After he had forced her to sign the paper, Cameron told her that she had been registered with a body called 'The Slave Company'. It was a powerful organization, he claimed, whose operatives had the house under constant surveillance. Any act of disobedience would mean certain death for Colleen's relatives, he said.

Because she had signed the contract, Colleen – known simply as 'K' – was given access to the rest of the Hooker house. This meant nothing in terms of freedom. Instead, she was now charged with performing the household chores. Cameron continued to torture Colleen and he often interrupted her busy day to whip her.

Events soon took another dramatic turn when Cameron took Colleen into the master bedroom. However, any hopes he might have had of a *ménage à trois* were dashed when Janice refused to join in. Nevertheless, Cameron raped Colleen after his wife had left the marriage bed.

Things changed again when the family moved to a mobile home on an acre of land they had bought just outside Red Bluff. Having lost his basement, Cameron kept Colleen captive in a new box that slid under his waterbed. As Colleen lay in her box, the

A TV crew visits the mobile home where the Hookers once lived

conception and birth of the Hookers' second child took place noisily above her.

Though Colleen spent more time in the box under the bed than in the coffin-like container at the old house, she was now allowed outside. She had contact with the neighbours and she even went jogging. It was only her fear of the Slave Company and what it might do to her family that prevented her from escaping.

Witnessing these examples of servitude, Cameron's confidence grew and his fantasies changed. In 1980, during the fourth year of captivity, he sent both his wife and his slave to a local bar to pick up men. When Colleen was not looking after the Hooker children, she was sent out into the streets of Reno and other communities to beg for money. Cameron's boldest move came when he had his slave write letters to her three sisters – they were the first signs they'd had that Colleen was still alive. Emboldened, he allowed a phone call and, eventually, a visit to her divorced parents in southern California.

On 20 March 1981, a thin, tired-looking Colleen was dropped off at her father's home.

She had been gone for almost four years. It was a pleasant, if tense, visit. Little was said because her family were wary of driving her away. On the following morning, not long after she had attended church

This leather face harness was produced as evidence in court

with her mother, Colleen was picked up by Cameron – or 'Mike' as he called himself. It was the name he had used three years earlier on the slave contract.

Back to square one

Colleen's return to the mobile home in Red Bluff marked yet another change in her circumstances. In many ways, it was a return to the treatment she had known when she had first been taken captive. Cameron bothered with her much less and the torturing became less frequent.

Colleen's days were now spent almost entirely in the box under the waterbed. Deprived of exercise and daylight, her hair began to fall out and she started to lose weight.

She listened as Cameron began talking to Janice about acquiring another slave – perhaps more than one. Cameron spent a good portion of the summer and autumn of 1983 digging a hole near the mobile home, so that a dungeon could be built. After he had installed flooring and walls, it became Colleen's home. However, the underground chamber soon flooded, so Colleen was returned to her box.

After that failed experiment, Cameron came to the conclusion that he needed to move to a bigger place before he abducted more slaves. In order to achieve his goal, he sent

Tenant Betty Hayes demonstrates where Colleen was imprisoned

Colleen to work at the local King's Lodge Motel. The young woman remained dutiful, telling co-workers nothing of her situation. Yet it was at the motel that Colleen's chains of captivity began to loosen. On 9 August 1984, she was picked up from work by Janice. The car trip home was anything but routine. Janice told Colleen that there was no Slave Company, no one was watching the mobile home and the contract was bogus. In short, every threat Cameron had used to keep her in bondage was a lie.

Tables turned

That evening, the two women planned Colleen's escape. By the next morning Colleen was on a bus to southern California, having been wired money by her father. Before leaving Red Bluff, she telephoned Cameron from the station. He cried when she told him that she was leaving. There would be more telephone calls in due course.

Although Colleen had told no one about her seven-year ordeal, she could not leave the Hookers behind. It was not long before she began calling Janice on a regular basis. She made 29 telephone calls in total, in which she encouraged Janice to leave Cameron. Colleen had grown bolder since she had discovered the truth about the Slave Company and she stood up to Cameron whenever he answered the phone. In tears, he pleaded with her to come back. The tables had turned.

After one abortive attempt, Janice did leave her husband, after making a full confession to her church minister, Pastor Dabney, who then telephoned the police. On 18 November, the Hookers were arrested. There would, however, be only one trial because Janice had been granted full immunity from prosecution in exchange for agreeing to testify against her husband. It took over ten months for Cameron's case to come to trial. He testified in his own defence, arguing that all sex acts with Colleen had been consensual. On 28 October 1985, Cameron Hooker was found guilty of kidnapping, rape and eight other offences. He was sentenced to a total of 104 years in prison.

Danger signs: When dating his wife Joyce, he tied her up, suspended her from a tree and beat her

----

Pattern of crime: Hooker's ritualistic, sadistic fantasies became a shared preoccupation with his initially submissive wife Janice

----

Breakthrough: Reported to police by local minister after wife's confession

----

Sentence: 104 years

THE SLAUGHTERWOMAN'S FEAST

Katherine Knight

Name: Katherine Knight

DOB: 24 October 1955

Profession: Slaughterhouse employee

Upbringing: Sexually abused by members of her family; father was alcoholic

Previous charges: Arrested for leaving her baby on a railway line; took hostages at knifepoint

Number of victims: 1

Katherine Knight once worked in Australian slaughterhouses where she discovered a talent for decapitating pigs. She used the very same knives from her work to murder her common-law husband. John Price was skinned and beheaded; portions of his buttocks were cut from what remained of his body. All this was in preparation for a stew intended for his children. But it was not the work of a madwoman; courts determined that Katherine was quite sane. She had planned the murder, knew that it was wrong and was well aware of the consequences of her grizzly actions.

Katherine Mary Knight was born on 24 October 1955 at Tenterfeld, New South Wales, one of many communities in which her father, Ken, had found employment as a slaughterhouse worker.

Kath lived a semi-transient life until 1969, when her family settled in Aberdeen, 170 miles (270 km) north of Sydney. The town may have been small – with just over 1,500 inhabitants – but the Knight family was fairly large. A twin, Kath was one of eight children.

Violent bully

Barely literate, she wasn't much of a student; Kath still made a mark at the schools she attended by being a violent bully. At the age of 16, following in the footsteps of her father, brother and twin sister, Kath became a slaughterhouse worker herself. The following year, she met and moved in with David

It was her partner's misfortune that Katherine Knight was destined to take the skills she had learnt in the slaughterhouse back home with her

Kellett, a 22-year-old truck driver. The couple married in 1974, a happy occasion that was marred when the bride, disappointed by his sexual performance on their wedding night, tried to strangle her groom.

As the relationship progressed, so too did the abuse. In what, by comparison, seems a trivial incident, Kath burned all David's clothing. Early in the marriage, he arrived at work with the imprint of an iron burned on to the side of his face. The truck driver once awoke to find his wife astride his chest holding a knife to his throat.

And yet, he stayed with Kath long enough to father, and witness the birth of, a daughter, Melissa,

born in 1976. It was a joyous occasion in an otherwise unpleasant and disturbing period.

'I never raised a finger against her,' David said, 'not even in self-defence. I just walked away.' Within two months he had done just that, leaving his wife for another woman.

In retaliation, Kath placed Melissa on railway tracks just minutes before a train was scheduled to pass. The baby was discovered and saved by a local drifter, and, incredibly, the mother suffered no repercussions.

Kath was not so lucky when, a few days later, she disfigured a 16-year-old girl's face with a butcher's knife. A stand-off ensued, during which Kath held a young boy hostage. She was placed in a psychiatric hospital, only to be released a few weeks later. There was a reunion with David, who worked to save what was left of the marriage.

Doomed

The attempt was doomed from the start. Despite the medication and therapy she'd received, Kath was, if anything, more violent. And yet, in 1980 the couple had a second daughter, Natasha.

It would have been understandable had David again walked away, yet it was Kath who ended the

> **Even more disturbingly, Knight took one of Dave's dogs, an 8-week-old puppy, and, making sure he was watching, killed the creature by cutting its throat**

relationship. He returned home one day to discover his house stripped of its contents and Kath, Melissa and Natasha gone.

In 1986, she began seeing a man named Dave Saunders, with whom she had a daughter, Sarah, the following year. Kath soon left her slaughterhouse job, citing a back injury. With Dave's help, and the aid of a significant compensation package, she bought a rundown house in an undesirable area of town, and, setting health concerns aside, began renovating and decorating. Kath's tastes were fairly unconventional: cow hides, steer horns, a stuffed baby deer, rusted animal traps and a scythe hung on a rope above her couch. And the pattern of her life

was unchanged. Kath cut up her boyfriend's clothes, vandalized his car, hit him with an iron, stabbed him with scissors and beat him with a frying pan until he was unconscious. Even more disturbingly, Kath took one of Dave's dogs, an 8-week-old puppy, and, making certain he was watching, killed the creature by cutting its throat.

As their relationship drew to an end, Kath took an overdose of sleeping pills and wound up in another psychiatric hospital. And yet, somehow, she managed to obtain an Apprehended Violence Order that kept Dave away from her and his child.

By May of 1990, Kath had moved on to another man. John Chillington, a cab driver, became another victim of her abuse. She smashed glasses grabbed from his face and destroyed his false teeth. Despite the drama, in 1991 the pair had a child, Eric, together.

In 1994, Kath dumped John for her final partner, John Charles Price, known as 'Pricey'. He was a well-liked man; even his former wife, with whom he'd had four children, spoke of him only in glowing terms.

After a little more than a year together, Kath abandoned her shoddy, bizarrely decorated home for Pricey's more tasteful, well-built bungalow. Even before moving in, the relationship had taken several bad turns. The pair had been seen fighting – typical behaviour for Kath, but very much out of character for Pricey.

Frustrated by Pricey's refusal to marry her, Kath presented a videotape to her boyfriend's employers depicting items allegedly stolen from his work. Though the goods featured, all well past their expiry dates, were probably scavenged from the trash, Pricey was fired – an abrupt end to 17 years of dedicated service. Kath and Pricey split up. But within a few months they were back together.

Unable to read or write, Pricey's employment

Left: John Price (front) with family: daughter Rebecca Rosemary holding baby, ex-wife Colleen and son Johnathon & his Hinder, Kris's sister. Son J. and his sister Rosemary hug after court

John Price (second from the left) and his original family in much happier times

options were extremely limited. Pricey sank into drink for a time, until, by chance, he happened upon a job at Bowditch and Partners Earth Moving. It was just the sort of break he needed. A year after being hired, Pricey was made supervisor.

He'd begun to share elements of his unhealthy relationship with the boys from work, telling them that Kath had a history of violence and that he wanted her out of the house. Pricey also claimed his wife could throw a punch as good as any man alive and that she'd once chased him with a knife. Pricey's stories were at odds with the woman known to his friends at work. The Kath they'd seen might

have been a bit of an odd bird, but to an outsider she seemed pleasant enough. By the early months of 2000, Pricey had begun making an effort to share his concerns.

On 21 February, he was forced to flee the house after Kath had grabbed a knife in an argument. Though some of Pricey's friends encouraged him to leave, he felt the need to stay in order to protect the children. Eight days later, during his noon-hour break, Pricey went to a local magistrate. He feared for his life and showed a wound he'd received when Kath had stabbed him. After returning to work, his boss offered him a place to stay, but Pricey declined.

Victims . . . John Price (above, left) with his son Johnathon. Right: Price's house and the scene of the gruesome supper (below)

John Price, seen here with his son Johnathon, was a typical product of smalltown Australia – a conscientious worker with a love of beer and 'cigs'

Eerie premonition

A family video, shot just a few hours later, captures Katherine singing nursery rhymes to her children. Her sole grandchild, a girl, sits on her lap. It was an out-of-character performance, complete with the peculiar message: 'I love all my children and I hope to see them again.' After the camera was switched off, she and the children enjoyed a dinner at a local Chinese restaurant. Again, it was something out of the ordinary. Kath told the children, 'I want it to be special.'

Aged 20, Natasha had a vague feeling of unease about the meaning of her mother's unusual behaviour. As Kath left to see Pricey, she said, 'I hope you are not going to kill Pricey and yourself.'

Later, Kath claimed that she had no recollection of the evening after having watched *Star Trek* at Pricey's house.

Much of what we now know is drawn from forensic evidence gathered at the scene. We know that at some point Kath donned a black negligee bought at a local charity shop. It's highly probable that she was wearing the flimsy garment when they had sex – it is certain that Kath had on the negligee when she began stabbing Pricey. The wounded man managed to make it outside his front door before being dragged back into the house, where the stabbing continued. The coroner determined that Pricey received at least 37 stab wounds, destroying nearly all of his major organs.

When Kath began skinning, beheading and otherwise carving up her lover is unknown, though cameras did manage to record her movements at 2.30 am, when she made a withdrawal from an ATM.

It was at Bowditch and Partners that the first concerns for Pricey were raised. Such was Pricey's dedication and reliability that at 7.45 am his boss phoned local police to report that he had not yet arrived at work.

The authorities visited Pricey's bungalow, forced the door and found his skin hanging in a doorway. The decapitated corpse was lying in the living room. Pricey's head was in a large pot, simmering away on the kitchen stove.

The dining room table held two servings of food, consisting of baked potato, pumpkin, courgette, cabbage, squash and generous portions of the cooked corpse.

Placement cards indicated that the two settings were intended for Pricey's children. Barely literate notes containing baseless allegations were addressed to the children. Having taken a mild overdose, the author, Kath, lay semi-comatose on the bed she and Pricey had once shared.

In October 2001, Kath admitted her guilt in Pricey's death. The following month she became the first woman in Australia to receive a life sentence without the possibility of parole. Speculation remains as to whether she ate any of the meal prepared from Pricey's body.

Danger signs: Battered a lover unconscious with a frying pan, then cut the throat of a puppy in front of him

Pattern of crime: Stabbed Price in the chest and grew increasingly vindictive towards him

Judge's summing-up: 'This was an appalling crime, almost beyond contemplation in a civilized society'

Sentence: Life imprisonment (never to be released)

Name: Ed Kemper

DOB: 18 December 1948

Profession: State Highway Department worker

Nickname: 'The Co-ed Killer'

Upbringing: Poor relationship with his mother who constantly belittled him; ran away from home as a teenager to visit his estranged father who rejected him

Description: Diagnosed with 'a personality trait disturbance, passive-aggressive type'; IQ of 136; height 6 ft 9 in (over 2 m)

Previous convictions: Sent to Atascadero State Hospital for shooting his grandmother and grandfather at the age of 14 – said he wanted to find out 'what it would feel like to shoot Grandma'

Number of victims: 10

Ed Kemper

It is sometimes claimed that serial killers want to be caught. Increasing sloppiness, risk-taking and taunting yet revealing letters sent to the authorities are often cited as proof. Ultimately, we cannot really know. However, it can be said with certainty that Edmund Kemper, the 'Co-Ed Killer', wanted to be caught, and that's down to the simple fact that he actually turned himself in.

Edmund Emil Kemper III was born on 18 December 1948 in Burbank, California, the home of the Walt Disney Company and Warner Brothers. An only son, he had one older and one younger sister. Kemper was named after his father, with whom he was extremely close. In 1957, his parents divorced, and his mother moved with the children to Helena, Montana. There, nearly 2,000 km (1,250 miles) away from his father, Kemper suffered his mother's emotional abuse. She would often lock him in the basement, thinking that he would molest his sisters. While still a child he began to torture and kill animals, and used his sisters' dolls in acting out aberrant sexual fantasies and situations. On more than one occasion, his younger sister found that her dolls had been decapitated. In a favourite childhood game

Kemper would dream of his own execution, enlisting one of his sisters to lead him to a pretend electric chair.

Not wanted

At the age of 13 he ran away from home and made his way back to California. His father, who had remarried, was somewhat less than pleased to see him. It was during the trip that Kemper learned he had a stepbrother – a boy who had replaced him in his father's affections. He was sent back to Montana, where he was equally unwelcome.

As a 14-year-old, he was sent to live with his paternal grandparents, Maude and Edmund Kemper, on their 17-acre ranch in North Fork, California. Despite his height, he was easily bullied. According to Kemper, his grandmother was another in a long list of tormentors. On the afternoon of 27 August 1964, the two argued and, taking the rifle given to him by his grandfather the previous Christmas, Kemper shot his grandmother once in the head and twice in the back. It was an impulsive act.

His grandfather arrived home and was shot as he got out of his car. Kemper would later say that he killed his grandfather to spare the old man the discovery of his dead wife, killed by his grandson.

After phoning his mother to tell her what he had done, Kemper called the local police and waited on the porch for their arrival. In custody he was diagnosed as having paranoid schizophrenia and sent to the Atascadero State Hospital for the Criminally Insane.

On his 21st birthday, 18 December 1969, against the wishes of several psychologists, he was released into his mother's care. She had moved back to California during her son's incarceration, and was now living in Santa Cruz. Kemper attended community college and received high marks. He became friendly with various members of the Santa Cruz Police Department. For a time he planned on becoming an officer, a dream that ended when he learned he was too tall. Now standing 6 ft 9 in, and weighing nearly 300 lb (136 kg, or over 20 stone), Kemper cut an imposing figure.

He worked at a number of jobs before settling into a position as a labourer with the California Division of Highways. Kemper wasn't good with money, but he managed to save enough to move out of his mother's home and share an apartment with a roommate. He also purchased a motorcycle, which played a part in two separate accidents. As a result of one of these, Kemper received a settlement of $15,000.

He used this money to buy a yellow Ford Galaxie, and began to cruise the area along the Pacific coast in search of female hitchhikers. By his own estimation, he generously provided rides to approximately 150 young women and girls, all the while slowly gathering items of sinister purpose in his trunk: knives, handcuffs, a blanket and plastic bags.

On 7 May 1972, he picked up his first victims, Mary Ann Pesce and Anita Luchessa, who were hitchhiking 170 miles (270 km) from Fresno to Stanford University. At first the girls felt themselves lucky, as Kemper told them he would drive all the way to Stanford. However, he soon turned off the highway and on

Victim Aiko Koo decided to hitchhike after tiring of waiting for a bus

Kemper being arraigned in 1973

to a deserted dirt road. There he stopped, killed both girls, and drove back to the highway with their bodies in his car boot. In a scene reminiscent of a movie cliché, Kemper was almost caught when, as he drove back to his apartment, the police pulled him over and issued a warning for a broken tail light.

Kemper arrived at his apartment to find that his roommate was out. He carried in both bodies, laid them on the floor of his bedroom and began to dissect them, taking photographs to mark his progress. He later admitted that he'd had sex with various severed parts. He disposed of the girls' bodies in the mountains, burying that of Pesce in a shallow grave which he marked in order to find it on future visits.

He continued to give lifts to women, often engaging in conversations about an unknown man who was murdering female hitchhikers. On 14 September, he raped and killed Aiko Koo, a 15-year-old girl who had decided to hitchhike after becoming tired of waiting for a bus. She, too, was taken to the apartment and dissected. The next day Kemper went before two psychiatrists, a requirement of his parole. As a result of the interview, it was concluded that he was no longer a danger. Later, he disposed of Koo's body parts outside Boulder Creek.

Escalation

The following January and February, Kemper killed three more women, two of whom he picked up at

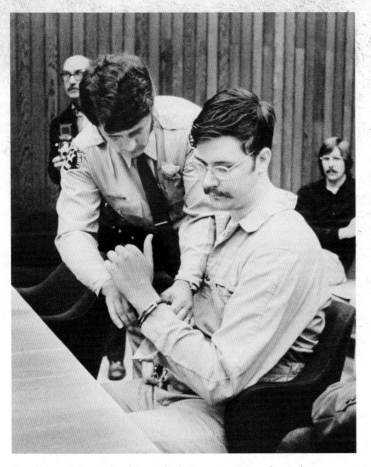

Even in court, it was hard to read what was on Kemper's mind

in Pueblo, Colorado, he called his old friends at the Santa Cruz Police Department and confessed to the murder of his mother, her friend and the six female hitchhikers. However, the officer who took the call, knowing Kemper, did not think him at all capable of the crimes, and considered the call a practical joke made in poor taste. It took several further phone calls to convince the Santa Cruz police that a visit to Mrs Kemper's house might be warranted.

On 7 May 1973, Kemper was charged with eight counts of first-degree murder. While awaiting trial, he twice attempted suicide. The trial began on 23 October and Kemper's plea of not guilty by reason of insanity was countered by three prosecution psychiatrists who declared him to be sane. In the end, he was found guilty on all eight counts.

He asked to be sentenced to death, but his childhood fantasy was denied. Kemper is currently serving a sentence of life imprisonment in the California State Medical Corrections Facility.

the University of California's Santa Cruz campus, where his mother worked. These same two women he dismembered and beheaded in his mother's home.

On 21 April 1973, Good Friday, Kemper killed his mother with a pick hammer as she slept. After decapitating her, he sexually assaulted the corpse. He placed the head on the mantelpiece and used it as a dartboard. He then invited over one of his mother's female friends, Sally Hallett, whom he strangled and beheaded. On Easter Sunday, he drove off eastwards in Hallett's car, listening for news reports of the murders he had committed on the radio. After driving approximately 1,500 miles (2,400 km) without hearing a word on his crimes, Kemper pulled off the road. From a phone booth

Danger signs: Cruelty to animals from an early age; as a child he liked to stage his own mock-execution

----

Pattern of crime: Picked up hitchhikers whom he strangled, stabbed or shot, then raped their headless bodies

----

Breakthrough: Turned himself in after murdering his mother – he had put her vocal chords down the garbage disposal... 'That seemed appropriate, as much as she'd bitched and screamed and yelled at me over so many years'

Sentence: Life imprisonment without the possibility of parole in Vaccaville, California's home for the criminally insane

----

THE CHARMER

Jack Unterweger

Name: Jack Unterweger

DOB: 16 August 1950

Profession: Television host, novelist and journalist

Upbringing: Illegitimate son of an American soldier and a prostitute; brought up by his alcoholic grandfather

Description: A handsome man whose looks concealed a sexually sadistic psychopath

Previous charges: Theft, assault and one previous murder conviction

Number of victims: 10 to 15

Jack Unterweger entered prison as an uneducated murderer and emerged a celebrated author. The toast of Vienna, he was feted and invited to openings and soirées – but his real interest was in murdering prostitutes.

He was born Johann Unterweger on 16 August 1950 to a prostitute in Judenburg, Austria. He never knew his father, nor did he even know the man's identity. However, it was generally assumed then, as now, that Unterweger's father was probably an American soldier. Abandoned at birth, for his first seven years he was raised in extreme poverty by an alcoholic grandfather in a one-room cabin.

From an early age Unterweger displayed a wild and unpredictable temper. At 16, he was arrested for the first time after having assaulted a woman. Tellingly, Unterweger's victim was a prostitute. Other crimes followed in quick succession; he was charged with stealing cars, burglary and receiving stolen property. He was also accused of having forced a woman into prostitution and taking all the proceeds.

On 11 December 1974, he and a prostitute named Barbara Scholz robbed the home of an 18-year-old German prostitute named Margaret Schäfer. Afterwards, Schäfer was taken by car into the woods, where Unterweger tied and beat her. Then he removed her clothes and demanded sex. When she refused, he hit her with a steel pipe and she was strangled with her own bra. He was quickly caught.

In his subsequent confession, Unterweger tried to defend his actions by saying that it was his mother whom he'd envisaged beating, and not Margaret Schäfer.

Locked up

Unterweger was sentenced to life in prison for the murder. Having received little in the way of

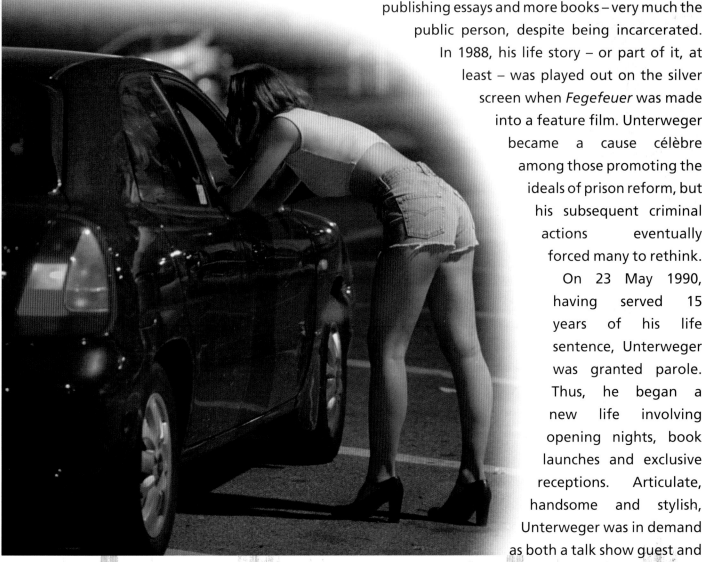

schooling as a child – he entered incarceration as an illiterate – he found prison could provide him with an education. His progress was dramatic. He soon learned to read and write, and developed an interest in the literary arts. In a short time, he was writing poetry, plays and short stories, as well as editing the prison's literary magazine.

In 1984, his first book, an autobiography entitled *Fegefeuer – eine Reise ins Zuchthaus* ('Purgatory: A Journey to the Penitentiary'), was published to great acclaim and went on to become a bestseller. Unterweger was soon giving interviews and publishing essays and more books – very much the public person, despite being incarcerated.

In 1988, his life story – or part of it, at least – was played out on the silver screen when *Fegefeuer* was made into a feature film. Unterweger became a cause célèbre among those promoting the ideals of prison reform, but his subsequent criminal actions eventually forced many to rethink.

On 23 May 1990, having served 15 years of his life sentence, Unterweger was granted parole. Thus, he began a new life involving opening nights, book launches and exclusive receptions. Articulate, handsome and stylish, Unterweger was in demand as both a talk show guest and

a dinner guest. His career as a writer seemed to go from one height to another; he was sought after as a journalist and his plays were being performed throughout Austria.

Before long, as a journalist, he was covering a beat he knew well: murder. Much of his writing concerned a number of prostitutes who had recently been murdered. He put both his past and celebrity to good use, moving freely through the streets. In his writing and in television pieces he berated the authorities for not having solved the crimes,

> ## *The body of Heidemarie Hammerer was discovered on New Year's Eve... it was apparent she had been strangled with a pair of tights*

asserting that there was a serial killer in Austria who was preying on prostitutes.

The first of these prostitutes, Brunhilde Masser, had last been seen alive on 26 October 1990 on the streets of Graz. Less than six weeks later, another prostitute, Heidemarie Hammerer, disappeared from Bregenz, near the border with Germany and Switzerland. Her body was discovered on New Year's Eve by two hikers. Upon inspection, it was apparent that she had been strangled with a pair of tights. Though she was fully clothed, it was after her death that she had been dressed. On 5 January 1991, Masser's body was found outside Ganz. Though badly decomposed, the corpse revealed that she too had been strangled with tights.

Unterweger enjoyed stepping into the celebrity spotlight

On 7 March, another Austrian prostitute, Elfriede Schrempf, disappeared. By this point the authorities were becoming extremely concerned. Since it is a legal occupation in Austria, prostitution has fewer dangers than in many other Western nations. In an average year, the country would suffer no more than one murdered prostitute. And yet, in little more than four months two prostitutes had been murdered and another had gone missing. Worries increased when Schrempf's family received two phone calls in which they were threatened by an

> **Looking at all the evidence, a team of investigators from Graz, Bregenz and Vienna concluded that the murders and disappearances were not the work of a serial killer, a finding with which Unterweger took issue**

anonymous man. Though unlisted, their number was one that Schrempf carried on her person.

On 5 October, hikers discovered Schrempf's remains in the woods outside Graz. Within a month, another four prostitutes would disappear from the streets of Vienna. Looking at all the evidence, a team of investigators from Graz, Bregenz and Vienna concluded that the murders and disappearances were not the work of a serial killer, a finding with which Unterweger took issue.

Another person who disagreed with the team's findings was August Schenner. A 70-year-old former investigator, Schenner had been involved in solving the 1974 murder of Margaret Schäfer, for which Unterweger had served his prison time. He noted that Schäfer had been strangled, as had another prostitute whom he had always suspected Unterweger of killing. And, of course, all the recent murders of prostitutes had been committed by means of strangulation. When the bodies of two of the missing prostitutes surfaced, both strangled, the authorities became convinced that they did indeed have a serial killer on their hands – and that he was most likely Jack Unterweger.

The celebrity author was placed under surveillance for three days. On the fourth day, Unterweger flew off to Los Angeles, where he was to write an article on crime in the city for an Austrian magazine. In his absence, the Austrian federal police tracked their suspect's movements since his release from prison. They discovered that he had been in Graz on the dates when Brunhilde Masser and Elfriede Schrempf had disappeared; in Bregenz when Heidemarie Hammerer had been murdered, and in Vienna when all four prostitutes had gone missing. They also learned that Unterweger had visited Prague in September 1990. A call to Czech authorities revealed that they had an unsolved murder of a young woman, Blanka Bockova, dating from that time. When found by the bank of the Vitava River, her body had a pair of grey stockings knotted around the neck.

Special knowledge

After he returned from Los Angeles, Unterweger was questioned by officers of the criminal investigation bureau. One of the officers already knew the suspect as he'd been interviewed by the celebrity author for one of the articles he'd written on the murders. Unterweger denied knowing any of the prostitutes, saying that his knowledge of their respective fates was limited to what he'd found through his work as a journalist. He was let go due to lack of evidence. Soon thereafter, he resumed his attacks in print for what he described as the mishandling of the case.

In their hunt for evidence, the police discovered that Unterweger had sold the car he'd first bought after his release from prison. With the permission of the new owner, they went through the vehicle and discovered a hair fragment which, through DNA testing, was shown to be that of Blanka Bockova.

With the hair sample, investigators now had enough to obtain a search warrant for Unterweger's apartment.

A call to the Los Angeles Police Department brought news that three prostitutes had been strangled during Unterweger's time in the city.

When Austrian police moved in to arrest Unterweger, they discovered that he had left the city, ostensibly to holiday with Bianca Mrak, his 18-year-old girlfriend. In reality, he was fleeing to avoid arrest. Unterweger managed to enter the United States by lying about his previous murder conviction. He settled with Mrak in Miami, from where he launched a campaign against the Austrian authorities. At the centre of his fight was the accusation that the police were fabricating evidence in an attempt to frame him. Connections in the media were called upon in an effort to have his version of events published.

On 27 February 1992, Unterweger was arrested by United States marshals after he picked up money that had been wired to him. They arrested him on the grounds that, in lying about his 1974 murder conviction, he had entered the country illegally. He fought deportation until he learned that California, the state in which he was suspected of murdering three prostitutes, had the death penalty.

On 28 May, he was returned to Austria. There Unterweger was subject to a law which permitted him to be charged for the murders he was accused of committing both inside and outside the country's borders – 11 in total. Awaiting trial, Unterweger gave interviews and wrote letters to the media in which he professed his innocence. He was convinced that the public was on his side. However, the tide had long since begun to turn; even his former friends in the media doubted his innocence. Unterweger went on trial in June 1994 with the conviction that his popularity and charm would win over the jury.

On 29 June 1994, Unterweger discovered his luck had run out when he was found guilty of all but two charges of murder. He was sentenced to life in prison without parole.

That evening Unterweger used the string of his prison jumpsuit to hang himself. The knot he tied was the very same one he'd used on his victims.

Danger signs: His charm could be replaced by sudden outbursts of violent temper; misogynistic tendencies from a young age

-----

Pattern of crime: A string of prostitutes were murdered in Austria and surrounding countries by very similar methods

-----

Breakthrough: Former investigator noticed that new murder cases matched Jack Unterweger's modus operandi

-----

Sentence: Life imprisonment without the possibility of parole (he committed suicide by hanging himself less than 24 hours after the verdict)

BORN FOR THE GALLOWS

Carl Panzram

Name: Carl Panzram

DOB: 28 June 1891

Profession: Professional thief and lifelong jailbird

Upbringing: Brought up on a farm; father left home when he was 7; became an alcoholic in his teens; hopped a train and ran away from home at 14

Description: Killer and rapist

Convictions: Sent off to reform school by his family at the age of 11; served time in nine states, including Sing Sing prison (NY)

Number of victims: 22

As the moment of his execution approached, when serial killer Carl Panzram was asked whether he had any last words, he is reported to have turned to his executioner and said: 'Hurry it up, you Hoosier bastard! I could kill ten men while you're fooling around!' It was probably not much of an exaggeration.

Much of what we know about Panzram comes from his autobiography, published 40 years after his death. It is a well-written and articulate account of his life; not at all what one would expect from someone with limited formal education. The man who would come to murder dozens was born to a Prussian immigrant couple on 28 June 1891 on a Minnesota farm near the Canadian border. He and his six siblings were raised in poverty, a situation made worse when his father deserted the family. This shameful act took place when Carl Panzram was 7 years old. A year later the boy was arrested for the very adult crime of being drunk and disorderly. He was soon committing burglary, and at the age of 11 was sent to the Minnesota State Training School, a reform institution. Panzram's claims, made late in life, that he was beaten and sexually abused, are probably true. That he also committed his first murder there, the victim being a 12-year-old boy, has not been verified. In July 1905, he burnt one

Making up for a childhood of deprivation, Panzram later fenced goods on the Lower East Side, NY and bought himself a yacht on the proceeds

of the school's buildings to the ground. Evidently, he wasn't a suspect in the destruction, as he was released just a few months later.

Murder in mind

He enrolled in another school, but was soon in conflict with one of the teachers. The dispute was elevated to such a point that Panzram brought a handgun to class, intending to murder the instructor in front of his fellow students. The scheme collapsed when the gun fell to the floor during a struggle. He left the

> **Any feeling of freedom the 14-year-old Panzram might have felt probably came to an end when he was gang-raped by four men. As revenge, he went on to sodomize more than 1,000 boys and men**

school and the family farm, and started 'riding the rails'. Any feeling of freedom the 14-year-old might have felt in this transient lifestyle probably came to an end when he was gang-raped by four men. For the rest of his 39 years, Panzram was enraged by the pain and humiliation he had suffered through the incident. As part of some warped idea of revenge, he went on to forcibly sodomize more than a thousand boys and men.

Mere months after having left the Minnesota State Training School, Panzram was again in reform school, again for having committed burglary.

He soon escaped with another inmate named Jimmie Benson. They remained together for a time, moving around the American Midwest, causing havoc, burgling houses and stealing from churches before setting them on fire.

After they split up, Panzram joined the United States Army. It was a strange choice of profession, one for which he was ill suited. During his brief stint in service, he was charged with insubordination, jailed numerous times for petty offences and, ultimately,

was found guilty on three counts of larceny. Panzram received a dishonourable discharge and on 20 April 1908 was sentenced to three years of hard labour at the United States Disciplinary Barracks at Fort Leavenworth in Kansas.

In prison, the 16-year-old Panzram was beaten and chained to a 50-pound metal ball which he was made to carry. He dreamed of escape, but found it impossible. It was only after serving his three-year sentence that he finally got out. Panzram returned to his old transient lifestyle, moving through Kansas, Texas, California, Oregon, Washington, Utah and

> ***In prison, the 16-year-old Panzram was beaten and chained to a 50-pound metal ball which he was made to carry. He dreamed of escape, but found it impossible...***

Idaho. He committed burglary, arson, robbery and rape. In his autobiography, Panzram writes that he spent all his spare change on bullets and for fun would take shots at farmers' windows and livestock.

Another story involves a railway policeman whom Panzram raped at gunpoint. He forced two hobos to witness the act and then recreate it themselves.

He was arrested many times and served a number of sentences under a variety of assumed names. After his second incarceration and escape from Oregon State Prison, Panzram made his way to the east coast. Ending up in New Haven, Connecticut

Prisoners at Fort Leavenworth Penitentiary where Panzram served time

in the summer of 1920, Panzram burgled the home of former United States president William H. Taft, the man who had once signed the paper sentencing him to three years in prison at Fort Leavenworth.

The haul from the Taft mansion far exceeded previous burglaries. After fencing the goods in Manhattan's Lower East Side, Panzram bought a yacht. He then sailed the East River, breaking into the yachts of the wealthy moored along his route. He took to hiring unemployed sailors as deckhands. In the evenings, he would drug his crew, sodomize them, shoot each in the head with a pistol stolen from the Taft house and throw their bodies overboard. After about three weeks, Panzram's routine came to an end when his yacht was caught in an August gale and sank. He swam to shore with two sailors, whom he never saw again.

Heart of darkness

Following a six-month sentence for burglary and possession of a loaded gun, Panzram stowed away on a ship bound for Angola. While in the employ of the Sinclair Oil Company he sodomized and murdered a young boy. He later hired six locals to act as guides and assist in a crocodile-hunting expedition. Once downriver, with crocodiles in sight, he shot all six and fed the men to the beasts. After travelling along the Congo River and robbing farmers on the Gold Coast, he made his way back

In Angola, Panzram shot six guides and fed them to crocodiles

across the Atlantic.

Following his return to the United States, Panzram continued where he left off, committing robbery, burglary and sodomy. These 'routine' crimes were punctuated by the murders of three boys; each was raped before being killed.

On 26 August 1923, Panzram broke into the Larchmont, New York, train depot and was going through the stored baggage when he was confronted by a policeman. He was sentenced to five years in prison, most of which was served at Clinton Prison in upstate New York. True to character, Panzram made no attempt to become a model prisoner. During his first months at Clinton he tried to firebomb the workshops, clubbed one of the guards on the back of the head and, of course, attempted to escape. This final act had consequences with which he would struggle for the rest of his life.

The incident began when Panzram failed in his attempt to climb a prison wall. He fell nearly 30 ft (10 m), landing on a concrete step. Though his ankles

> *During his first months at Clinton he tried to firebomb the workshops, clubbed one of the guards on the back of the head and, of course, attempted to escape*

and legs were broken and his spine severely injured, he received no medical attention for 14 months. The months of agony Panzram endured intensified his hatred and he began to draw up elaborate plans to kill on a mass scale. One scheme involved blowing up a railway tunnel, then releasing poison gas into the area of the wreck.

> **Standing before his new warden on that first day, Panzram warned, 'I'll kill the first man that bothers me'**

One-man crime wave

When he was finally released from Clinton, in July 1928, Panzram emerged a crippled man. However, his diminished capacity did nothing to prevent his return to crime. During the first two weeks of freedom, he averaged approximately one burglary each day. More seriously, on 26 July 1928, he strangled a man during a robbery in Philadelphia. By August, Panzram was again in custody. Perhaps realizing that he would never again leave prison, he confessed to 22 murders, including those of two of the three boys in the summer of 1923.

On 12 November, he went on trial for burglary and housebreaking. Acting in his own defence, he used the courtroom as a stage from which to scare the jury and threaten witnesses. By the end of the day he had been found guilty on all counts and was sentenced to a total of 25 years in prison.

On 1 February 1929, he arrived at the United States Penitentiary at Leavenworth, Kansas. It was an area of the country he knew well; 20 years earlier he had served time at the nearby military prison. Standing before his new warden on that first day, Panzram warned, 'I'll kill the first man that bothers me.'

True to his word, on 20 June 1929, Panzram took an iron bar and brought it down with force on the head of Robert Warnke, his supervisor in the prison laundry. When the other prisoners attempted to escape, Panzram began chasing them around the room, breaking bones.

He was tried for Warnke's murder on 14 April 1930. Again, he undertook his own defence, smugly challenging the prosecutor to find him guilty. It wasn't a difficult challenge. When the judge sentenced Panzram to hang, he was threatened by the condemned man.

On 5 September 1930, Panzram was hanged. Many organizations had worked to prevent the execution, much to Panzram's annoyance. Nine months before his death, he wrote to one such organization, the Society for the Abolishment of Capital Punishment: 'The only thanks you and your kind will ever get from me for your efforts on my behalf is that I wish you all had one neck and that I had my hands on it.'

Danger signs: As a teenager, committed arson and fantasized about mass murder

Pattern of crime: Trapped in a vicious circle of committing violent crime and being imprisoned; his passion was to see churches burn

Breakthrough: Captured during a break-in

Last words: [to his executioner] 'Hurry it up, you Hoosier bastard! I could kill ten men while you're fooling around!'

Sentence: The death penalty

'ATROCIOUS BUT NECESSARY ACTIONS'

Anders Breivik

Name: Anders Behring Breivik

DOB: 13 February 1979

Profession: Bogus farmer

Aliases: Andrew Berwick, Sigurd Jorsalfare, Andersnordic

Category: Spree killer

Previous convictions: None

Number of victims: 77 killed, 153 injured

On the afternoon of 22 July 2011, a curious compendium titled *2083 – A European Declaration of Independence* was emailed to over a thousand recipients around the globe. Its author was a complete unknown, but by the end of the day he would be famous – not for his writing, but as the worst spree killer in world history.

Anders Behring Breivik was born on 13 February 1979 in Oslo, but lived most of his earliest days in London, where his father, an economist, worked as a diplomat for the Royal Norwegian Embassy. At the age of 1, his parents divorced, setting off a custody battle that

his father lost. Still an infant, Breivik returned with his mother, a nurse, to Oslo. Although she was soon remarried, to a Norwegian Army officer, Breivik would later criticize what he perceived as an absence of the masculine in his childhood home. In his writings, he disparages his mother for his 'matriarchal upbringing', adding 'it completely lacked discipline and has contributed to feminizing me to a certain degree.'

Anecdotal evidence shows Breivik to have been an intelligent, caring boy, one who was quick to defend others against bullying. However, his behaviour changed markedly in adolescence. Over a two-year period, so Breivik claims, he engaged in a one-man 'war' against Oslo's public transit company, causing £700,000 ($956,000) in property damage. His evenings were spent running around the city with friends, committing acts of vandalism. At the age of 16, Breivik was caught spray-painting graffiti on the exterior wall of a building, an act that brought an end to his relationship with his father. The two have had no contact since.

Though the stepson of an army officer, Breivik was declared 'unfit for service' in Norway's mandatory conscription assessment. The reason for this surprising judgement has yet to be disclosed; Breivik told friends a story that he'd received an exemption to care for his sickly mother. However, a possible explanation is his use of anabolic steroids, a drug that he'd been taking since his teenage years in an effort to bulk up. Breivik was a man obsessed with his appearance.

Utoya Island was Breivik's ultimate destination

No girlfriends

In 2000, at the age of 21, he flew off to the United States to have cosmetic surgery on his forehead, nose and chin. Unmarried at 32, Breivik considered himself a most desirable bachelor, and boasted frequently of his conquests, yet not one of his acquaintances can remember him ever having had a girlfriend.

'When it comes to girls,' Breivik wrote in his journal, 'I'm tempted – especially these days, after training and I'm feeling fantastic. But I try to avoid entanglements, because they may complicate my plans and put the whole operation in jeopardy.'

The operation he referred to was part of a nine-year plan that culminated on that horrible day in July 2011. According to Breivik, work began in 2002

> *By 2009, Breivik was back in business. He set up a company, which was nothing more than a cover to buy large quantities of fertilizer and other chemicals used in bomb-making*

with the establishment of a computer programming business that was intended to raise funds. Instead, the company went bankrupt, forcing him to move back to his mother's house. This humiliating setback seems to have brought on a period of relative inactivity. By 2009, however, Breivik was back in business. He set up a company, Breivik Geofarm, which was nothing more than a cover so that he might buy large quantities of fertilizer and other chemicals used in bomb-making without raising suspicions. The next year, after a failed attempt at buying illegal weapons in Prague, he purchased a semi-automatic Glock pistol and a Ruger Mini-14 semi-automatic carbine through legal channels.

Breivik murdered with these guns, but his first victims on 22 July 2011 were killed with a car bomb planted in his Volkswagen Crafter. That afternoon, he drove the automobile into the government quarter of Oslo, taking care to park it in front of the building housing the Office of the Prime Minister, the Minister of Justice and Police and several other high-ranking government ministers. At 3:22 pm, the car bomb exploded, shattering windows, and setting the ground floor of the building on fire. Though Labour Prime Minister Jens Stoltenberg, thought to have been a

A photo taken from a helicopter showing Breivik next to several bodies

chief target of the attack, survived without a scratch, the explosion killed eight people and left 11 more with critical injuries.

Things could have been much worse. It's curious that through all Breivik's years of planning, he'd never taken into account the fact that July is the month Norwegians go on holiday. What's more, he'd chosen to carry out his attack late on a Friday afternoon, a time when most government employees had already left for the weekend.

During the mayhem in downtown Oslo, Breivik changed into a fake police uniform, made his way some 40 km (25 miles) to the shores of Lake Tyrifjorden, and caught a ferry to the island of Utoya. His destination was a summer camp that was held annually by the youth wing of the Norwegian Labour Party. By the time he arrived – 4:45, one hour and 23 minutes after the Oslo blast – news of the tragedy had already been announced to the camp staff and roughly 600 teenagers on the island. Breivik appeared as he presented himself: a police officer who had come to ensure that the 26-acre island was secure. After first asking people to gather around so that he could speak with them, Breivik opened fire. He shot indiscriminately,

apparently intent on killing as many people as possible. Breivik's bullets struck people as they took to the lake, hoping to swim to safety.

Indiscriminate slaughter

It wasn't until 32 minutes after the shooting began that police on the mainland were aware of something taking place on Utoya Island. Their delayed response is a matter of investigation. They waited until the Beredskapstropen, a special counter-terrorism unit, arrived from Oslo, before making the crossing. The boat that they sailed on was so overloaded that it nearly sank before reaching the island. Even before they left shore, Breivik placed a phone call to surrender, only to change his mind. The killing continued until 6:26 pm – one hour and 24 minutes after it had begun – when the gunman made a second call. He was apprehended by the Beredskapstropen eight minutes later.

In all, Breivik killed 69 people on Utoya Island and its surrounding waters. Many of the survivors escaped with their lives by swimming to areas that

Fascistic image of Breivik from his personal website

Breivik revisits the scene of his crime to provide police with evidence

murderer rails against multiculturalism and what he sees as opening the door to the Islamization of Europe. Portraying himself as a knight, Breivik calls on other white Europeans to wage a religious war against Muslims and Marxists. His ultimate goal, as reflected in the title of the document, was the deportation of all followers of Islam from Europe by 2083.

'A majority of the people I know support my views,' he writes, 'they are just apathetic. They know that there will be a confrontation one day, but they don't care because it will most likely not happen within the next two decades.'

Breivik appeared in Oslo District Court three days after the attack. Facing charges of terrorism, the accused entered a not guilty plea, adding that he did not recognize the system under which he would be tried. The arraignment was held in camera, due to fears that he might somehow use the venue to communicate with compatriots. At time of writing, Breivik is being held in solitary confinement. It is expected that his trial will soon begin. Further charges may be added.

were only accessible from the lake, while others hid in a schoolhouse, which the gunman chose not to enter. Some survivors played dead, even after being shot for a second time. Still others were rescued by vacationers and others with boats, who risked coming under fire from the shore.

Breivik claimed a total of 77 lives with his two attacks; a further 153 people were injured. The dead ranged in age from 14 to 61, with a median age of just 18 years. He'd killed 55 teenagers.

Anders Breivik has acknowledged that he committed the bombing in Oslo and the shootings on Utoya, but has denied guilt. In his words, both events involved 'atrocious but necessary actions'. These four words came from his lawyer; Breivik has not yet stood trial. Much of the gunman's motivation can be gleaned through *2083 – A European Declaration of Independence*, the 1,513-page document that he released to the world just 90 minutes before setting off the Oslo bomb. In this collection of writings, much of it plagiarized from others, Breivik argues against feminism and for a return to a patriarchy that he felt was lacking in his own upbringing. The

Preparations: Purchase of guns, chemicals and fertilizer

Danger signs: Vandalism committed as a teenager; manifesto posted online just prior to killings

Behaviour in court: Defiant

Plea: Not guilty

Victim statement: 'If one man can show so much hate, think how much love we could show, standing together.'

ARMAGEDDON MAN

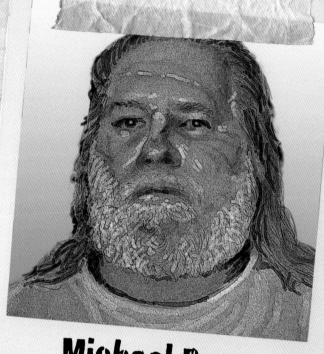

Michael Ryan

Name: Michael Ryan

DOB: 3 August 1948

Profession: Trucker

Description: Right-wing survivalist, white supremacist and cult leader

Previous convictions: Officials from three states raided the farm where he lived and found stolen weapons and 150,000 rounds of ammunition

Number of victims: 2

Michael Ryan was always keen to share his violent fantasies. At social gatherings he would often go on about being a Mafia hitman or a CIA operative. Not that this overweight truck driver was either, mind you: it was just that he wanted to be like those people. Ryan dreamed of blowing up buildings or becoming an assassin, but in the end he killed no one. Instead, he got other people to do it for him.

There was really nothing in Michael Ryan's background that would have appealed to the CIA recruiters. He was a high school drop-out, he had a violent temper, he liked to get into fights and he was a regular marijuana user. On top of all that, he also had a fondness for drink, though this did not prevent him from becoming a truck driver.

One victim of Ryan's violent behaviour was his wife Ruth. They got married in 1968, a few months after his 20th birthday. Ruth was small and slight, so she was no match for her husband, who stood 6 ft 2 in tall and weighed 220 lb (100 kg). Dennis, their only child, was also a recipient of Ryan's kicks and punches.

Then, one evening in May 1982, Ryan found God. This momentous meeting took place during a lecture given by the Reverend James Wickstrom in Hiawatha, Kansas. The pastor's words were unlike anything Ryan had ever heard in the Baptist church of his youth. Wickstrom told his audience that Anglo-Saxons were the true Israelites, that Jews controlled the banks and that a day of reckoning was on the horizon. Invoking the ancient name for God, he declared: 'Yahweh is a god of war! He came not in peace, but to send a sword.'

'Remember,' the pastor told the crowd, 'Yahweh said it's okay to kill, but thou shalt not murder. You must kill the enemy of Yahweh – that is dictated!'

Indoctrination

Ryan heard more than talk about religion that evening. Wickstrom was one of the leading figures in a group dedicated to the 'return of white Anglo-Saxon Christians to the rightful control of America'. The Posse Comitatus, as they called themselves, railed against the state and the federal government because they believed that government should only exist at the county level. These beliefs were tied up with Wickstrom's interpretations of the Bible.

After the talk, Ryan met Wickstrom for the first time. It was a brief encounter, but it made a big impression. 'You are a true Israelite!' the preacher exclaimed. Six months passed before the two men met again. This time, the location – a Best Western motel room – was much more intimate. It was there that

Wickstrom made Ryan believe he was an archangel fighting for Yahweh, 'god of war'

Wickstrom convinced Ryan that he possessed the ability – or the 'power' – to receive advice from God on all daily matters, no matter how trivial and seemingly inconsequential.

Driving home after the meeting, Ryan was like a man possessed.

'This is one of the most important things to happen in my life,' he told his brother-in-law Steve Patterson. 'I am beginning to see why I need to be here in this life.'

Over the following months, Ryan immersed himself in Wickstrom's teachings. He listened to cassette tapes of the cleric's sermons and he studied his pamphlets.

Ryan also attended Bible meetings hosted by Posse Comitatus members, but he came away disappointed.

It seemed that the farming families who had opened up their homes were more interested in discussing taxes, agricultural policy and politics than Yahweh as a god of war.

The Battle of Armageddon, mankind's final epic struggle, became Ryan's focus. With great conviction, he argued that the event would take place in Kansas.

It was all a bit much, even for those who followed the teachings of the Reverend Wickstrom.

Ryan prepared for the coming battle between good and evil with military-style drills and practice

People also grew tired of Ryan's constant bragging. He would go on and on about having lost two toes while serving with the Green Berets in Vietnam, when in reality every day of his 34 years had been spent in the United States. It was true that Ryan had *tried* to join the army, but he had been turned down on medical grounds. And those two missing toes? They were the result of a self-inflicted wound, an accident that had taken place when Ryan had discharged a rifle in the back of his grandfather's pick-up truck.

> ## Ryan took Rick Stice's wife, Lisa, to Kansas City, where he told her Yahweh had decreed she was to be one of his wives

But some people were taken in by Ryan's lies about life as a Green Beret. Hog breeder Jimmy Haverkamp was one of them. Haverkamp had renounced his Catholic upbringing to follow the Reverend Wickstrom and he would also become Ryan's first follower. The hog breeder was soon joined by other converts, including recently-widowed farmer Rick Stice. Heavily in debt and facing bankruptcy, Stice was attracted by the anti-government rhetoric of the Posse Comitatus and he was very impressed by Ryan's closeness to Wickstrom.

The three men even visited the minister in his modest home, after which Michael Ryan told them that his Christian name was no accident – he was the very embodiment of the archangel Michael, the field commander in the Army of God.

Ryan and his followers prepared for the coming conflict by robbing banks. Money was required to construct the bunker from which the Battle of Armageddon would be fought. As the months went by, Ryan gradually began to distance himself from Wickstrom. Eventually, he severed ties with the Posse Comitatus. Its founder was devoting too much of his time to politics and not enough to Yahweh. By early 1984 Ryan had over a dozen followers, including Haverkamp's sister Cheryl, whom he had taken as a second wife. The group moved on to the 80-acre Stice farm, just outside the small, isolated village of Rulo in the southeast corner of Nebraska. It was here that Ryan's male followers would prepare for the coming battle between good and evil.

Ryan staged military-type drills and stockpiled weapons, much to the distress of the neighbouring farmers. They complained to the authorities in vain – as far as anyone could tell, Ryan and his followers were breaking no laws. But this was still Stice's farm. The hog farmer had not been sure about allowing Ryan to use his land, but he had eventually agreed to his leader's request. Now he was beginning to regret his decision. The situation was made all the more tense by the fact that Stice's youngest son Luke despised Ryan. In turn, Ryan declared that the 5-year-old was 'of Satan'.

Things would only get worse for Stice. Only months earlier, Ryan had blessed the marriage of Stice and his new wife Lisa, but now he was trying to tear them apart. As 1984 came to a close, Ryan took Lisa to Kansas City, where he told her that Yahweh had decreed that she should leave her husband and be one of his wives. It did not matter that she was pregnant, because the unborn child was not Stice's – it was the result of an immaculate conception. Convinced that her role had been ordained by Yahweh, Lisa put up no resistance.

Shortly afterwards, Ryan announced that Yahweh had given him a gift of slaves – Stice and his son

> **Luke had been placed in a trailer, where he was suffering daily torture at Ryan's hands. The religious leader would spit in the boy's face and flick cigarette ash in his mouth. The boy died in the night after Ryan threw him into a bookcase**

Luke. There was a third slave, a former hardware store employee named James Thimm. Just days before, Ryan's 26-year-old follower had dared to question his leader's policies. After listening to Thimm's hesitant words, Ryan became livid.

'You need to get the f**k out of here if you're talkin' like that! Yahweh doesn't want Satan's people on this farm, bud, you're a proselyte! There's only one place for you… that's in hell. You better think about leaving!'

That last suggestion was the best advice Ryan ever gave the young man, but he did not take it. Now it was too late.

Luke was the first person to suffer at Ryan's hands. He beat the boy, stripped off his clothing and made him roll around in the cold February snow. Then he made him put a pistol in his mouth and pull the trigger. The barrel was empty.

After that, Ryan shot the boy in the arm, claiming that it was Yahweh who had pulled the trigger. Stice fled the farm in terror. When he returned four days later he was tortured and shackled. Try as he might, he could not save his son's life.

The boy had been placed in a trailer, where he was suffering daily torture at Ryan's hands. In addition to regular beatings and whippings, the religious leader would spit in the boy's face and flick cigarette ash into his mouth. The end of Luke's young life came when Ryan threw him into a bookcase.

'Yahweh does not want us to take Luke to a hospital,' Ryan announced.

The boy died during the night.

Shot in the face

James Thimm, who was confined to another trailer, was shot in the face by Ryan's son Dennis. He was wasting away, yet he was forced to join Stice in digging Luke's grave.

In the days that followed Thimm was beaten, whipped and sodomized with the handle of a shovel. Throughout all of this misery he asked for Yahweh's forgiveness. His life ended in the hog shed – the building he had come to consider home. After his hands had been tied to an overhead bar with baling wire, Thimm was whipped by Ryan's male followers as their leader watched. When he was taken down, Ryan picked up a Ruger .22 pistol and began shooting off his fingers.

After a break for lunch, Ryan ordered Thimm's murderers to return and resume his torture.

'Yahweh wants me to show you how we skinned people in Vietnam,' he announced.

Using razor blades and a pair of pliers, Ryan proceeded to strip James Thimm's skin from his body, making certain to show his victim each bloody piece of flesh. His son, Dennis, was an eager assistant. They broke Thimm's legs next. Ryan then began kicking his slave in the head, before jumping up and down on the young man's chest. According to Ryan, Yahweh wanted James Thimm dead by dinner time. The deadline was easily met.

On 18 August, the authorities found the grave

As James Thimm and Luke Stice found out, the hog farm in winter was a grim place to meet your end

that contained the bodies of James Thimm and Luke Stice. Ryan, his son Dennis and Timothy Haverkamp, brother of James, were promptly arrested. After being found guilty of second-degree murder, Dennis Ryan and Timothy Haverkamp were sentenced to life imprisonment.

A jury convicted Ryan of first-degree murder on 10 April 1986. As he waited to be sentenced, the cult leader was charged with murdering Luke Stice. In this case, he was found guilty of second-degree murder. Ryan was condemned to die in the electric chair, but moved on to Death Row and spent more than two decades cheating death.

Danger signs: Members of his cult stockpiled weapons and vitamins, styling themselves 'True Israelites'

Pattern of crime: Ryan wrote '666' on a 5-year-old's head and called him 'child of Satan', later murdering him; another victim was chained up in a pig shed and made to have sex with a goat

Plea for the defence: 'I thought that was what was to be done.'

Sentence: The death penalty

THE CASE OF THE TOXIC MILKSHAKES

Nancy Kissel

Name: Nancy Kissel

Profession: Homemaker and volunteer

Upbringing: Comfortable, upper middle class

Description: Outgoing and demanding

Previous convictions: None

Number of victims: 1

Nancy and Robert Kissel moved in together shortly after they met in 1987. Two years later they married: the late AIDS activist Alison Gertz was maid of honour. At the time, Robert was studying for a master's degree in finance at New York University. Nancy had two degrees of her own – in business and design – but she took three humdrum jobs to support the household.

After graduating in 1991, Robert set out on a trajectory that would have brought him earnings of well over $3,000,000 a year within a decade. He began his dramatic rise in New York at the investment bank Lazard Frères, before moving on to the Goldman Sachs Group. In 1997 he was transferred to Hong Kong. The Kissels then became prominent members of the American expatriate community. It should have been an enviable life – many outsiders thought it was. The Kissels and their two children settled into a luxurious suite at the exclusive Hong Kong Parkview. Robert worked and prospered, eventually joining Merrill Lynch, and Nancy did voluntary work. She assisted at the Hong Kong International School and the family's synagogue. In 1998, the couple were blessed with another child.

However, despite appearances, Nancy would later claim that her years in Hong Kong had been extremely unhappy. If what she claimed was true then the SARS epidemic of 2003 was the answer to her prayers. In March of that year, Nancy and her children joined the stream of Americans who were

Hong Kong, where the persistence of the SARS epidemic gave Kissel an excuse to head back to Vermont

> **The Kissels became prominent members of the American expatriate community in Hong Kong. It should have been an enviable life...**

fleeing Hong Kong for the relative safety of the United States. Leaving Robert to his work at Merrill Lynch, she travelled to the family's holiday home in the shadow of Stratton Mountain, Vermont.

As the months passed and the epidemic worsened, Nancy made the decision to have an elaborate home theatre system installed. It was as a result of this desire for escapism that she met a twice-divorced electrical repairman named Michael Del Priore.

Before long, Nancy and Del Priore began having an affair. With Robert many thousands of miles away in Hong Kong, they were able to enjoy much of the summer together. Nancy bought her lover a $5,000 wristwatch, which was perhaps an unusual possession for a man who lived in a trailer park.

By August the SARS crisis had abated, so Nancy and the children were back in their Hong Kong Parkview suite. The marriage continued as normal, but Robert must have noticed a difference in his wife's behaviour.

Suspecting that his wife was having an affair, he hired a private investigator. It took little effort to uncover the relationship, yet no physical evidence could be obtained.

Shortly afterwards, Robert again contacted the private investigator. This time, though, he was asking for a bit of advice. The banker said he had recently drunk a glass of single malt scotch, but it had not tasted right. After a few sips he had felt 'woozy and disoriented'. The detective advised Robert to have a sample of the scotch analyzed, but the banker failed to do so.

Nancy became fearful that her husband was on to her. She hid her calls to Michael by getting her mobile phone bills sent to the Hong Kong International School. However, her caution was no match for her husband's determination. Robert had spy software installed on all of the family's computers so that he could monitor Nancy's email and Internet use. He saw that his wife had been using search engines for such terms as 'drug overdose', 'sleeping pills' and 'medication causing heart attack'. And yet, despite all these findings, Robert would not act. The most he did was tell his friend David Noh, a colleague at Merrill Lynch, that he was worried about being poisoned.

The drinks Kissel made for her husband packed a real punch

A cocktail of drugs

On 2 November, Andrew Tanzer, a Hong Kong Parkview neighbour, dropped his daughter off to play at the Kissels' suite. As he got ready to return to his home, Tanzer and Robert were offered pink-coloured milkshakes, which they both drank. By the time Tanzer returned to his suite he felt heavy with sleep, so he lay down on the couch. His wife was unable to rouse him for a while, though he later recovered somewhat. He drifted in and out of sleep until dinner time. Tanzer's behaviour then became even more unusual. First of all he appeared disorientated and then he acted in a childlike manner by displaying an almost insatiable appetite. Before falling asleep for the evening, he lost control of himself and soiled the furniture. On the following day, Tanzer found that he could remember next to nothing of what had taken place after he had left the Kissels' home.

> **The milkshake that the two men had drunk had been laced with six medications, five of which had recently been prescribed to Nancy, including Rohypnol, the 'date rape drug'**

Disturbing though Tanzer's experience had been, Robert Kissel's night had been much worse. When Andrew Tanzer woke up the next morning, the investment banker had been dead for many hours. The milkshake that the two men had drunk had been laced with six medications, five of which had been recently prescribed to Nancy.

These were Stilnox, a sleeping pill; Amitryptaline, an antidepressant; Dextropropoxythene, a painkiller; Lorivan, a sedative; and Rohypnol, better known as the 'date rape drug'. Robert would have reacted to the concoction in much the same way as Andrew had. The difference was that Mrs Kissel had taken the opportunity to murder Robert while he was incapacitated.

At five o'clock in the afternoon, a tired and sleepy-sounding Robert spoke to David Noh in preparation for a company conference call. Though the event took place only 30 minutes later, Robert did not participate – it seems that he had forgotten all about it. Curiously, Robert was on the line to his secretary less than half an hour after missing the conference call. It was the last time anyone at Merrill Lynch heard from Robert. At some point in the evening of 2 November Nancy Kissel picked up an eight-pound (3.6 kg) figurine and gave Robert five blows to the head. She hit him so hard that she cracked his skull wide open.

Robert's corpse remained in the suite for three days, though it was out of sight of the Kissel children. As it lay locked in the master bedroom, Nancy began spreading conflicting stories. She told a doctor that Robert had assaulted her on 2 November. A maid was shown injuries that he was supposed to have made. Robert was now staying in a hotel, she said. His disappearance was noticed almost immediately. David Noh was disturbed to discover that he was unable to contact the investment banker: Robert was not answering his phone. Another friend, Bryna O'Shea, was also worried. Aware of Robert's marital difficulties she had made calls to several hotels, thinking that he might have moved out of the Parkview. On 6 November, after comparing notes with Bryna, David notified the authorities.

Closing in

Investigators interviewed Nancy at the Parkview apartment just a few hours later. It was her second contact with the police that day. That morning she had made a complaint against Robert. She had claimed that he had assaulted her five days earlier, when she had refused to have sex with him. Her weak attempt at creating a smokescreen had been in vain. The Parkview maintenance men had told

Kissel and family members outside the Hong Kong High Court during the trial

going to have to face a jury that was composed entirely of ethnic Chinese.

The prosecution presented Nancy as an adulterous wife who had murdered her husband so that she could run off with her lover. The evidence against the widow Kissel was almost overwhelming: the prescription medicine that had been present in the milkshake; the testimony of Andrew Tanzer; and the rolled-up carpet that the maintenance men had moved to the storage room. Faced with these findings, and more, Nancy's solicitor fell back on British law. This allows the defendant to enter a plea of diminished responsibility if the circumstances surrounding the crime are extraordinary.

Nancy began testifying on 1 August 2005. It was then that she provided a detailed description of a man who was unrecognizable to the other American expatriates.

She claimed that her husband had been addicted to cocaine, that he was an alcoholic and that he would beat her and force her to have oral and anal sex almost every single night. The sex had been so rough, she said, that Robert had once broken one of her ribs. Nancy then explained away her Internet research on sleeping pills, drug overdoses and medications that might cause heart attacks. She claimed that she had done it at a time when she had considered killing herself.

The blackening of Robert's character continued. Nancy told the court that her deceased husband had

the police that on the previous day Mrs Kissel had asked them to move an oriental rug to her storage locker. It had proved to be so heavy that four men had been required for the job. With this news, the investigators left the building to obtain a search warrant.

As midnight approached, the police entered the Parkview storage room. It took them next to no time to find Robert's corpse. As they suspected, it had been hidden within the rolled-up rug, though not very well. Robert's remains had been sealed in two layers of plastic – and yet there was an omnipresent stench of death. Shortly before three o'clock in the morning, Nancy was arrested and charged with murdering her husband. Throughout all of her years in Hong Kong, Nancy had been immersed in the American expatriate community. Now she was been a bad parent. When she had been pregnant with their youngest child, Robert had wanted labour to be induced so that the birth would not conflict with a business trip he had planned.

At another point, he had become so irrationally angry with one of his daughters for playing loudly while he had been on the telephone that he had broken the girl's arm.

Nancy admitted to the affair with the Vermont repairman, though she claimed that she would never have left her husband. According to Nancy, the same could not be said for Robert. She told the court that on the day her husband had died he had stood in the doorway of the kitchen as she was making the pink milkshakes. While holding a baseball bat 'for protection', Robert had told his wife that he had filed for divorce. He also said that

> *Kissel claimed her husband was addicted to cocaine, that he was an alcoholic and that he would beat her and force her to have oral and anal sex almost every single night*

he would be taking the children, because Nancy was not fit to care for them.

Nancy then testified that she and her husband had begun to fight. She said that Robert had struck her and had then tried to rape her.

The figurine had been grabbed in self-defence, but she had then hit him on the head with it. Robert had sat stunned but when Nancy had tried to help he would not let her.

Instead, he had taken the baseball bat and swung it at her legs. At that point, she fell silent. She claimed that she could remember nothing more of the evening or of the days that followed.

The prosecution took issue with Nancy's testimony. They asked her why she had never mentioned the abuse she had suffered to anyone, doctors included. And why was it that no one had seen any signs of injury?

Nancy's story fell apart even more when the Kissels' maid testified that the broken arm had been nothing to do with Robert. Indeed, he had not even been home when the accident had occurred.

On the evening of 1 September 2005, the jury reached a unanimous decision – Nancy was found guilty of murder.

Under Hong Kong law the mandatory sentence is life imprisonment. Because their mother has been found guilty of the murder of their father, the three Kissel children will one day inherit Robert Kissel's estate, which is estimated at $18 million.

Danger signs: Conducted an adulterous affair; began to believe her husband supected

Breakthrough: Police interview with maintenance men who had recently moved an oriental rug to the Kissel storage locker

Plea for the defence: 'There's nothing psychiatrically wrong with me. I'm not suffering from a mental illness. Depression? Yes. Feeling sad, feeling remorseful? Yes. Suffering from something tragic? Yes'

Sentence: Life imprisonment

INDEX

PICTURE CREDITS

AP/Press Association Images: 78, 79

Barrington Barber: 7, 104

Bill Stoneham: 114

Corbis: 8 (HO/Reuters), 20 (Andy Clark/Reuters), 23 (Handout/Reuters), 24 (Christopher J. Morris), 31 (Pat Dollins/ZUMA Press), 36 (Fred Prouser/Reuters), 38 (HO/Reuters), 48, 52 (Georges de Keerle/Sygma), 54, 58 right, 59, 60, 62, 63, 64, 66, 72, 81 right (Bettmann), 89 (Bernd Vogel), 94 (Bettmann), 96 left and right (Bettmann), 97 (Bettmann), 98 (Vienna Report Agency/Sygma), 99 (Gilles Fonlupt/Sygma), 100-101 (Vienna Report Agency/Sygma), 106-107, 110 (Jon Are Berg Jacobsen/Aftenposte/epa), 111 (Britta Pedersen/epa), 112 top (Marius Arnesen/epa), 113 (Trond Soldberg/epa), 121 (Bobby Yip/Reuters)

Getty Images: 51

PA Archive/Press Association Images: 18, 112 bottom

PA Photos: 41, 58 left, 83 (Walt Zebosky), 120, 124

Reuters: 11

Shutterstock: 9, 14, 16, 27, 28, 39, 55, 68, 70, 95, 108, 116, 119, 122

SoulRider: 222 (flickrname): 45

Topfoto: 44, 47

U. S. Air Force: 37

ZUMA Press: 26, 29, 74 (Paul Tooley), 80 (Paul Tooley), 81 left (Paul Tooley), 82, 84, 85, 86 (Sacramento Bee), 87 (Sacramento Bee)

Cover images: (clockwise from top left) Zuma, PA Archive, Corbis (x2)

We have made every effort to contact the copyright holders of the photographs and illustrations in this book. Any oversights or omissions will be corrected in future editions.